ALTERNATIVE SOLUTIONS TO DEVELOPING-COUNTRY DEBT PROBLEMS

ALTERNATIVE SOLUTIONS TO DEVELOPING- COUNTRY DEBT PROBLEMS

Edited by
Rudiger Dornbusch
John H. Makin
David Zlowe

American Enterprise Institute for Public Policy Research
Washington, D.C.

Distributed by arrangement with

University Press of America
4720 Boston Way
Lanham, MD 20706

3 Henrietta Street
London WC2E 8LU England

Chapter 2 in this volume, "Developing-Country Debt Problems after Seven Years," by John H. Makin, first appeared as the May 1989 issue of the *AEI Economist*.

ISBN 0-8447-3696-1 (pbk.)

AEI Studies 494

Printed in the United States of America

TP

Contents

ACKNOWLEDGMENTS   ix

CONTRIBUTORS   xi

1   INTRODUCTION
    Rudiger Dornbusch and John H. Makin   1

                        PART ONE
              APPROACHES TO THE DEBT PROBLEM

2   DEVELOPING-COUNTRY DEBT PROBLEMS AFTER SEVEN YEARS
    John H. Makin   9

3   REDUCING TRANSFERS FROM DEBTOR COUNTRIES
    Rudiger Dornbusch   21

4   MARKET-BASED APPROACHES TO DEBT REDUCTION
    Paul R. Krugman   43

5   INSTITUTIONAL APPROACHES TO DEBT RELIEF
    Eugene H. Rotberg   65

                        PART TWO
      EVALUATIONS OF APPROACHES TO THE DEBT PROBLEM

6   CAPITAL FLIGHT AND REFLIGHT
    Allan H. Meltzer   71

7   THE KEY QUESTION IS THE BARGAINING
    Stanley Fischer   75

8   THE NEED FOR DEBT CONCESSIONS AND FORGIVENESS
Jim Kolbe   79

9   THE VIEW OF THE BANKING COMMUNITY
John B. Haseltine   83

10   NOT ONE DEBT PROBLEM BUT HUNDREDS
Slade Gorton   87

11   DIFFERENT TREATMENT OF DIFFERENT COUNTRIES?
A Discussion   91

12   DEBT REDUCTION, DEBT-SERVICE REDUCTION,
AND NEW MONEY
David C. Mulford   97

13   MAKING THE BEST USE OF RESOURCES
A Discussion   105

APPENDIX : THIRD WORLD DEBT
Nicholas F. Brady   115

NOTES   123

INDEX   125

LIST OF TABLES

1–1. External Financing of Countries Experiencing Debt-Service Difficulties, 1981–1988   3
2–1. Debt Burden of Fifteen Debtor Countries, 1981 and 1988   15
2–2. Market Valuation of Developing-Country Debt, Selected Dates, 1985–1989   16
2–3. American Banks' Exposure to Developing-Country Debt, 1987 and 1988   18
3–1. External Debt as Percentage of Gross Domestic Product for Latin America and Seventeen Indebted

Countries, Selected Years, 1980–1987 23

3–2. Economic Growth, Inflation, Investment, and Transfer of Interest in Latin America, 1970–1988 24

3–3. Estimates of Capital Flight for Six Latin American Countries, 1976–1987 29

3–4. Problem Debtors in Latin America, the Philippines, and Seventeen Countries, 1988 30

3–5. U.S. Bank Exposure in Latin America, 1985 and 1988 30

4–1. Secondary Prices on Debt of Developing Countries, April 1989 43

4–2. Welfare Effects of Alternative Buyback Schemes of Developing-Country Debt 45

4–3. Effects of a Hypothetical Buyback of Externally Financed Developing-Country Debt 48

4–4. Effects of a Hypothetical Pure Debt Swap of New Developing-Country Debt for Old, with New Debt Senior to Old Debt 50

4–5. Hypothetical Debt Swap of New Developing-Country Debt for Old, with Incentive Effects 53

4–6. Effects of a Domestically Financed Hypothetical Buyback of Developing-Country Debt, Assuming Complete Appropriability 56

4–7. "Brady Plan" for Developing-Country Debt without Seniority for Guaranteed Debt 59

4–8. "Brady Plan" for Developing-Country Debt with Guaranteed Debt Seniority 60

LIST OF FIGURES

1–1. Secondary Market Prices of External Debt in Argentina and Mexico, January 1986–March 1989 4

3–1. Latin America's per Capita Real Income, 1980–1988 22

3–2. Latin America's External Transfer of Resources, 1977-1989 25

4–1. The Debt Laffer Curve 52

Acknowledgments

This volume is based on the proceedings of the Alternative Solutions to Developing-Country Debt Problems Conference, held April 18, 1989. The conference and volume were made possible by a grant from the Rockefeller Foundation, and the editors wish to thank the foundation for their generous support. We also thank the American Enterprise Institute for allowing us to reprint the May 1989 *AEI Economist* written by John H. Makin. Secretary Brady's March 10, 1989, speech, which is in the public domain, is included as an appendix.

The editors thank Chris DeMuth, David Gerson, Isabel Davidov, Pat Ford, Madeline Milligan, Meriam Walker, Shirley Blanchard, and Don Flick of the American Enterprise Institute for their assistance in making the conference a success. The Miller Reporting Company, Inc., transcribed the conference proceedings.

R. D.

J. H. M.

D. A. Z.

Contributors

RUDIGER DORNBUSCH is the Ford International Professor of Economics at MIT. He has held positions at the Fundação Getulio Vargas in Rio de Janeiro and elsewhere. Dr. Dornbusch is an associate editor of the *Quarterly Journal of Economics* and the *Journal of International Economics*. His many publications include two of the standard texts in economics: *Macroeconomics*, with Stanley Fischer; and *Economics*, with Dr. Fischer and Richard Schmalensee. Dr. Dornbusch received his Ph.D. in economics from the University of Chicago.

STANLEY FISCHER is vice-president for development economics and chief economist of the World Bank. He is on leave from MIT, where he is a professor of economics. Dr. Fischer has taught at the University of Chicago and Hebrew University in Jerusalem. He is coauthor of the classic texts *Macroeconomics*, with Rudiger Dornbusch, and *Economics*, with Dr. Dornbusch and Richard Schmalensee. Dr. Fischer is editor of *Macroeconomic Annual* of the National Bureau of Economic Research. He holds a Ph.D. in economics from MIT.

SLADE GORTON (R-Wash.) is a member of the Senate Commerce, Armed Services, and Agriculture Committees. He participated for two years in the Twentieth Century Fund's study of third world debt. Before his first election to the Senate in 1980, he served as Washington state attorney general for twelve years.

JOHN B. HASELTINE is a senior vice-president of the First National Bank of Chicago and is currently on assignment as the director of banking at the Institute of International Finance. He has an M.B.A. from the European Institute of Business Administration in Fontainebleau, France.

JIM KOLBE (R-Ariz.) is in his second term in the House of Representatives. He serves on the Congressional Border Caucus, which is concerned with issues relevant to both Mexico and the United States. As a member of the Appropriations Committee, he is on the Subcommittee on Military Construction and the Subcommittee on Commerce, Justice, State, and the Judiciary.

PAUL R. KRUGMAN is a professor of economics at MIT, a position he has held since 1984. Previously, he was an international policy economist for the Council of Economic Advisers. Dr. Krugman is a research associate with the National Bureau of Economic Research and serves on the board of advisers of the Institute for International Economics. He has published extensively on international economics and trade, including *International Economics: Theory and Policy*, with Maurice Obstfeld, and *Market Structure and Trade Policy*, with Elhanan Helpman, which is forthcoming from the MIT Press. He received his Ph.D. in economics from MIT.

JOHN H. MAKIN is a resident scholar at the American Enterprise Institute, where he has been director of the institute's fiscal policy studies program since 1984. Previously, he was professor of economics and director of the Institute for Economic Research at the University of Washington. Dr. Makin has written on trade policy, international economics, and general economics, including *The Global Debt Crisis*; *Sharing World Leadership? A New Era for America and Japan*; and other books and periodicals. He received his Ph.D. in economics from the University of Chicago.

ALLAN H. MELTZER is a visiting scholar at the American Enterprise Institute and is the University Professor and John M. Olin Professor of Political Economy and Public Policy at Carnegie-Mellon University. From 1988 to 1989, Dr. Meltzer was an acting member of the Council of Economic Advisers. He has been a visiting professor at Harvard University, the University of Chicago, the University of Rochester, and the Fundação Getulio Vargas in Rio de Janeiro, among others. Dr. Meltzer is the author of several books and more than 150 papers on economic theory and policy. He is also a founder and cochairman of the Shadow Open Market Committee.

DAVID C. MULFORD is the under secretary of the Treasury for international affairs, where he is directing international debt strategies for the administration. Dr. Mulford was an assistant secretary of the Treasury for international affairs from 1984 to 1989. Earlier, he spent twenty years in the international investment banking business, including service as senior adviser at the Saudi Arabian Monetary Agency and as a director of Merrill Lynch & Co., Inc., for ten years. Dr. Mulford received his doctorate from Oxford University.

EUGENE H. ROTBERG is executive vice-president of Merrill Lynch & Co., Inc. He joined the firm in 1987 after serving as vice-president and treasurer of the World Bank for nineteen years. Mr. Rotberg was responsible for the borrowing of resources from governments and from capital markets to finance the World Bank's lending program to developing countries and for investment of the World Bank's liquid reserves.

DAVID ZLOWE is a researcher at the American Enterprise Institute where he studies U.S. federal budget issues and international trade. He has worked on infrastructure financing projects for the Senate Committee on the Budget and the Port Authority of New York and New Jersey. Mr. Zlowe also worked at the Hudson Institute on budget issues. He received his M.B.A. and Master of Public Management from the University of Maryland.

1

Introduction

Rudiger Dornbusch and John H. Makin

In August 1982 the developing-country debt crisis erupted. In the aftermath of imprudent borrowing and an unfavorable world macroeconomic environment, Mexico was unable to pay the interest on its debts to commercial banks, the International Monetary Fund (IMF), and the World Bank. Soon, a host of countries, from Brazil to Argentina, from Bolivia to Venezuela and the Philippines, followed. Today the World Bank counts seventeen countries experiencing debt-service difficulties. The list is not shrinking; the prospect of normality, as a result of a favorable world economy and serious domestic adjustment, is simply not on the horizon.

The onset of the 1982 debt crisis came on the heels of a decade-long $700 billion surge in lending to a diverse group of developing countries. The lenders were a small group of the world's largest banks, a few governments, and international agencies like the World Bank and the International Monetary Fund.

Seven years after the debt crisis onset, total external debts of developing countries have reached $1.3 trillion. Much of the $600 billion in new lending, especially since 1986, has come from official sources with commercial banks reluctant to add to their exposure to developing-country loans. The poor performance of some debtor economies coupled with the fact that official debts are in most cases senior to commercial bank loans (they must be paid first) has resulted in reductions in the market value of developing-country debt to an average of 35 percent of its face value. Mexican debt is valued at about forty-five cents per dollar of face value; Argentina's debt, about twenty cents; and Brazil's, about thirty cents.

The disputes in 1989 concern how much to write down debts of each country and what the mixture of private and official accommodation should be (the Brady approach), not over how to enable countries ultimately to repay all of their debts (the Baker approach). The primary difficulty in resolving the disputes, beyond reaching agreement be-

1

tween borrower and lender on the amount to be written down, is the problem of devising schemes that do not reward irresponsible behavior by borrowers and lenders. Borrowers whose loans have fallen most in value because of mismanagement cannot be awarded larger write-downs than responsible borrowers. On the lending side, it must be recognized that any officially sponsored measures that cause the value of third world debt to rise will confer the greatest rewards in terms of portfolio appreciation and thereby lower costs of capital upon banks that have been least active in reducing their exposure to developing-country debt. These "moral hazard" problems will be overcome only by compromises on all sides of negotiations and a case-by-case approach to negotiations between borrowers and lenders.

A diagnosis of the 1982 debt crisis reveals three reasons for the debt-service problems:

• excessive borrowing, with resources used to finance deficits and consumption with persistent trade deficits at overvalued exchange rates
• overlending by banks that acted on the apparent belief that sovereign debt need not meet ordinary banking tests
• a sharp deterioration in the world economic environment with a fall in commodity prices, a strengthening of the dollar until 1986, record high interest rates, and a decline in demand for manufactured goods

In response to this diagnosis, muddling through seemed the appropriate response. There was every expectation that the recession in the world economy would be followed by recovery and that high interest rates would decline in the aftermath of successful disinflation in the United States. Commodity prices would show a cyclical recovery as would developing-country exports. On the home front, adjustment efforts in debtor countries could not fail to improve their ability to service debts. Budget trimming and more competitive real exchange rates would enhance exports, curb imports, and thus help to close the foreign exchange gap. And if the confidence in these factors were not enough, there was an even stronger argument. If debtor countries did not make efforts to stay within the system, they would lose access to the world capital market. That approach, however, would condemn their growth prospects because, without external capital to supplement domestic saving, the prospects for capital formation would be dim.

Today, seven years later, the optimism of 1982 is no longer warranted. Many of the debtor countries have undergone a massive deterioration of their economies, and the clock has been turned back on social progress by a decade or more. Moreover, if the 1980s were a lost decade, the prospects for the 1990s are not assuredly better. It is true that there are exceptions. Chile has been able to establish sound economics, although social progress, by some standards, has been limited. Colombia (with the help of drug money and conservative finance) has avoided high inflation and falling incomes. Mexico, at a frightening cost in real wage cuts and output decline, has forced the budget into balance. The record of these countries, however, has as a counterpart hyperinflation and the destruction of social stability in Argentina, Brazil, and Peru. Populism is rampant, and the ability and willingness to service debts recede by the day.

Since 1982 debt service has been achieved by a combination of involuntary lending by commercial banks, increasing participation by multilateral institutions, and trade surpluses in debtor countries. Table 1-1 illustrates this in a striking fashion; in the period 1983–1988 commercial banks did not increase their exposure. The increase in exposure in the early phase of involuntary lending has been undone by various forms of swap programs since then.

While commercial banks withdrew from lending, to the extent that they could, official agencies were increasingly drawn into the lending process. Under U.S. Treasury policy, there was always a good excuse for another loan, be it to Argentina or to Brazil, even if the fundamentals of economic reform did not support the case. The World Bank estimates that the exposure of multilateral organizations alone increased from 8 to 16 percent of the liabilities of highly indebted countries.

It is difficult to tell at what point the expectation of an easy return to normality gave way to the realization that the muddling-through process was not a winning strategy. A clear turning point, however, is the Baker plan, announced in fall 1985. The plan was a response to the lack of growth in Latin America and to the increasing difficulty in structuring "new money" packages, that is, in making up for the difference

TABLE 1-1

EXTERNAL FINANCING OF COUNTRIES EXPERIENCING
DEBT-SERVICE DIFFICULTIES, 1981–1988
(billions of dollars; annual average)

	1981–1982	1983–1988	1988
Current Account	-84.2	-21.9	-20.6
Interest	-56.5	-57.9	-59.2
Trade balance	-22.3	25.4	24.3
Net External Borrowing	73.7	23.7	12.9
From commercial banks	56.8	0.03	-12.4

SOURCE: *IMF World Economic Outlook*, April 1989.

FIGURE 1-1

SECONDARY MARKET PRICES OF EXTERNAL DEBT IN ARGENTINA
AND MEXICO, JANUARY 1986–MARCH 1989

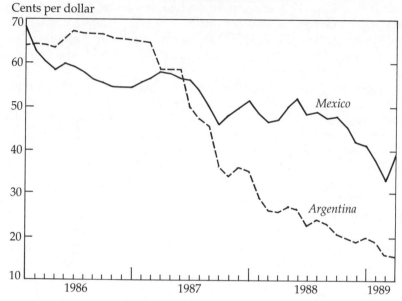

between interest due and what debtor countries were generating by trade surpluses. Banks were called upon to participate more spontaneously, and debtor countries were urged to undertake progrowth, market-oriented adjustment programs. Banks did not become more eager to lend, and debtor countries did not find in the plan the carrots or sticks that would motivate them to change policies. Soon, moratoriums ensued, first in Brazil and then in a host of other countries.

In the face of obvious failure, the administration insisted that there was no alternative. And that view was widespread among those who tried to hold together the process—no easy answers. Even though secondary market prices were deteriorating (see figure 1–1) muddling through remained the answer. Thus, in 1988, Secretary Baker approvingly quoted Paul Volcker's support for the status quo:

> I note with interest that just last week, Paul Volcker, in comments on the debt strategy, reportedly observed that "there's been a tendency among academics and the media to pronounce the plan dead. They've had six years to think of another approach," he added, "and they haven't been able to come up with one. The strategy remains," he concluded, "the only effective method in sight."

The riots and killings in Venezuela, the deterioration in Mexico's ability (political and economic) to sustain debt service, and, possibly, second thoughts about the political implications of a stark deterioration of Latin America's prosperity ultimately forced a change in strategy. Secretary Brady announced on March 10, 1989, an important new strategy, a sharp change from the status quo. The elements of the Brady plan were the following four:

• The plan recognizedthat debt *reduction* was essential; debts at existing levels could not be paid without putting social and economic stability in jeopardy. From growing out of debt, the policy shifted to getting rid of debt.
• Resources would be provided (on a case-by-case basis) to support market-based debt reduction through buybacks or interest support. The multilateral institutions and Japan (not the taxpayer) would be the source.
• Multilaterals should disburse, even if agreements with banks had not been concluded. Arrears were pronounced acceptable.
• Debtor countries would have to contribute by continued adjustment and by offering access to foreign investment, specifically in the form of debt-equity swaps and other menu items.

The initial expectations, chiefly those of debtor countries and the naive, of a major debt write-off were very rapidly squashed. The numbers shrank as it became apparent that the Brady plan had been prepared without sufficient attention to incentives operating on borrowers and lenders. Foreign governments did not believe there was a case for major public underwriting of debt reduction, and Japan, while committing resources, did not offer enough to make the problems go away. The multilaterals shrank from the opportunity to offer massive resources.

The Brady plan still lacks final form. It appears, though, that a total of $20 billion might be available from public sources. Negotiations with Mexico are bogged down: the country cannot pay—import liberalization has eaten up the trade surplus! Banks are unwilling to take write-offs without guarantees on the remaining portion. The Treasury has run out of bright ideas for other parties to foot the bill. With a major part of Mexico's financing requirements unfilled, with strategic posturing of all parties, and with debt-service fatigue pervasive, a 1930s-style suspension of debt service until further notice is not impossible, and not even undesirable from the standpoint of some participants in debt negotiations although still unthinkable to others.

This volume offers a concise update on critical issues facing borrowers and lenders, both in the public and in the private sectors, as the debt crisis moves into its eighth year. Perspectives of leading analysts, commercial banks, borrowing countries, and the U.S. Treasury are included in the essays, the panel discussion, and the address to the conference by Treasury Under Secretary David Mulford. Secretary Brady's speech appears here as the latest major initiative to deal with the aging debt crisis (see appendix).

If we are ultimately able to find ways to manage the stubborn problems faced by borrowers and lenders alike, capital markets in developing countries could once again serve as conduits for investment in the many economically viable projects now extant but delayed by uncertainty over the disposition of outstanding debts.

PART ONE
Approaches to the Debt Problem

2

Developing-Country Debt Problems after Seven Years

John H. Makin

During the almost seven years that have passed since August 1982 when a "debt crisis" surfaced, the crisis has become a collection of problems almost as numerous as the many different countries still struggling with heavy external—and internal—debts.

Since May 1987 when Citicorp's John Reed took his bank and most other banks out of the business of making additional loans to debtor countries, the primary method of managing the debt problem has been to have official institutions or governments lend to debtor countries the means to make debt-service payments on their loans. The result has not been helpful to commercial banks and, owing to the market value of claims on debtor countries, has in fact been harmful to them. The reason for this result is that although official loans have provided the means to service debt, they have simultaneously added to the total debt of developing countries and increased the share of that debt that is senior to the claims of the commercial banks.

The loans of the International Monetary Fund (IMF) and World Bank must be serviced and paid before commercial bank loans. As a result, countries that have not been growing rapidly enough to add prudently to their debts have done so with debts to official institutions that leave commercial banks further back in the queue of creditors. The value of commercial bank loans to debtor countries has, as a result, been cut in half since 1986.

The Brady Plan

To his credit, U.S. Treasury Secretary Nicholas Brady appears to have recognized that the process of official lending and further debt accumulation by countries whose internal and external debts are rising steadily cannot constructively continue. The economic growth and reforms hoped for under this approach have either not occurred or not pro-

9

gressed rapidly enough to satisfy either the borrowing countries or the lending banks and official institutions, not to mention investors who are quickly moving their money out of most debtor countries (capital flight) or marking down the value of existing loans to developing countries.

To recognize a problem is not to solve it, however, and the so-called Brady proposal still has a long way to go before it takes a specific form as a plan or suggests some way of lessening debt problems. The Brady proposal for debt reduction, now blessed by President Bush, moves American policy on third world debt to its third stage. His predecessor once removed, Donald Regan, simply denied the existence of a problem for either lending banks or borrowing countries while his immediate predecessor, James Baker, acknowledged a problem for both borrowers and lenders but clung to the vain hope that growth and new loans tied to structural reforms in debtor countries would make loan write-downs unnecessary while turning the sluggish economies of Latin America into the likes of the newly industrialized Asian countries.

Secretary Baker's hope was undercut by two realities. The market value of developing-country debt fell steadily from an average of about two-thirds of book value in September 1985 when Mr. Baker received great applause for acknowledging the existence of the debt problem to about one-third of book value today. The drop in the market value of debt accelerated in mid-1987 after Citicorp Chairman Reed stunned his banking colleagues by setting aside loss revenues equal to about 25 percent of his bank's holdings of third world debt. Mr. Reed's bold move and the follow-on by most money center banks signaled that private lenders were no longer prepared to lend to debtor countries the wherewithal to service their loans in exchange for maintaining the fiction that the loans were worth their full book value.

Mr. Reed was only acknowledging what had already been reflected in the prices of traded stocks of money center banks while underscoring the fact that Citicorp was better able than most of its competitors to absorb the losses on third world debt. He also invalidated the no write-down approach of the Baker plan.

Since 1987 most commercial banks have managed to dilute further their nominal exposure to third world debt through a combination of growth, loan sales, and debt-for-equity conversions. Meanwhile, major debtors—except Chile—led by Peru, Brazil, Argentina, and Venezuela have increasingly resorted to inflation finance and other measures that have not, judged by the continued plunge in the market's valuation of their debt, increased their creditworthiness.

At the same time political unrest—as recently evidenced by riots in Venezuela that killed 200 people protesting gasoline and transport subsidies—has jolted official Washington to recall Henry Kissinger's reinvocation earlier this year of the *glasnost*-diminished Communist threat: "Latin American populism is the last refuge of traditional Marxism. It has been impervious to Glasnost and Perestroika. . . .If a new approach to the debt problem does not emerge through imaginative U.S. leadership, it will be shaped in the crucible of confrontation."[1] The riots that erupted in Venezuela, coupled with pressure from the Mexican government, sparked visions of Kissinger's "crucible of confrontation" at the Treasury Department.

The official transposition of the third world debt issue from an economic to a political problem, spiced with the ever-pungent undertone of a "Communist threat," lent a note of irony to Secretary Brady's debt reduction speech delivered in the ornate banquet room at the State Department. There was the new Treasury secretary suggesting a new direction for American policy on an issue that had moved into the domain of the State Department, while the new secretary of state, James Baker, author of the approach to third world debt that was being abandoned, was traveling in the Middle East.

The kindly interpretation of this strange juxtaposition of events would be that Mr. Baker was too deeply engrossed in learning his new responsibilities as secretary of state to continue a heavy involvement in the debt issue. Still, the new and more urgent geopolitical cast of the third world debt problem leads one to ask when and how the new secretary of state will endorse abandonment of his "initiative" on third world debt undertaken in the interest of hemispheric security.

While the political-economic significance of the debt problem may have been upgraded, its details remain unchanged and still, even after Mr. Brady's speech and subsequent negotiations among governments and international institutions, unaddressed.

A group of developing countries, mostly in Latin America, owes about $500 billion in debts to commercial banks and official institutions. About $300 billion of the $500 billion is owed to commercial banks. The economic circumstances of the debtor countries vary tremendously, but collectively they are becoming unable or unwilling to pay the interest on the debt, let alone the principal.

Mr. Kissinger's "Latin American populism" is a vision of a state of affairs that threatens to disrupt the stability of the Western Hemisphere. Further, debt-squeezed Latin American countries are not the good customers for U.S. exports that they once were, partly because until the debt problem is resolved, no one will lend them the money to finance imports from the United States.

What Debtor Countries Want

The American banks have reserved, swapped into equity, or sold off about a third or $100 billion of their loans to debtor countries. Collectively, they probably would be willing to write down Latin American debts by about that $100 billion and also give proportionate interest relief, provided that the diminished interest and principal are guaranteed.

The problem is that the debtor countries want more. They point out that the market value of their debt to the commercial banks averages only about a third of its book value and claim that they should get debt reduction equivalent to two-thirds of their liabilities to the banks or about $100 billion more than the banks are prepared to grant.

There is an obvious flaw in the reasoning of the debtor countries. The countries whose debts are worth the least are those who have performed the worst in servicing their debts. If debt reduction is made proportional to the reduction in the market's valuation of a country's debt, a canny finance minister would simply repudiate the debt and obtain a 100 percent debt write-down. History is full of cases where nations so relieved of their debt are not precluded for very long from receiving new loans.

A Debt Facility

Most plans to resolve the third world debt problem revolve around bringing together the commercial banks and the debtor countries on the amount of debt to be written down. The commercial banks might even accept write-downs of greater than one-third if they received airtight guarantees that the amount of debt left after the write-down would be serviced promptly and reliably. Such a guarantee would have to be offered either by international institutions like the IMF and the World Bank or by a new "debt facility" that would take over administration of debtor country loans and would have resources available to make good on their commitments should debtor countries be unable to do so.

Suppose a debt facility could offer the commercial banks 50 cents on the dollar for their third world loans. This would represent splitting the difference between the approximate 67 cents on the dollar against which the banks have reserved and the 33 cents on the dollar at which the market has valued third world loans. In exchange for an additional $40–50 billion in write-downs, the banks would be guaranteed interest and principal on their remaining loans.

A problem arises with financing and operating the debt facility. At 50 cents on the dollar, the debt facility would on average be offering a 50 percent premium over market on developing-country loans. They would be guaranteeing the payment of interest and principal on the loans at a level significantly above the market assessment of the prospect for such payment.

Obviously, the debt facility would have to be provided with substantial equity capital if it were to offer credible guarantees on developing-country debt, even at 50 percent of its book value. Since the debt facility would be guaranteeing debtor country liabilities at 50 percent or about $50 billion above market value, its potential demand for equity, even if the existing valuation of debtor country liabilities does not deteriorate further, would be $50 billion.

The initial investment by supporters of the debt facility, which would obviously include leading industrial countries like the United States, Japan, Germany, and others in the G7, need not be $50 billion. The size of the initial equity subscription depends on the horizon over which the debt problem is to be solved.

A ten-year time horizon would require, for the sake of prudence, an initial equity subscription of about $20 billion. That amount, compounded at 10 percent annually, would be worth $50 billion after ten years. The $50 billion would be available to make good on debt facility guarantees under the conservative assumption that the current valuation of third world debt is correct. About half that amount or a $10 billion subscription would be appropriate over a seventeen-year horizon.

Suppose that between $10 billion and $20 billion of financial commitment is required to set up a credible debt facility. Where would the money come from? American resources have already been strained by the requirements of a domestic debt facility to deal with savings and loan problems. European banks have already written off most of the developing-country debt and so are not overly inclined to contribute heavily to such a debt facility.

This leaves Japan. There is a widespread perception that in its new role as an economic leader Japan may wish to shoulder more international responsibility and undertake a significant part of the burden of funding a debt facility. Indeed, Japan's interest in Mr. Brady's speech was so intense that its contents had been released in Tokyo by the Ministry of Finance even before his remarks were delivered in Washington.

Former Japanese Finance Minister Miyazawa made clear the terms on which Japan is prepared to offer more "burden sharing" on third world debt in exchange for more "power sharing." Japan would likely be prepared to commit as much as $10 billion to funding a debt facility in exchange for representation at international institutions like the IMF and the World Bank that is proportional to its enlarged financial contribution to those institutions. More voting power for Japan at the IMF and World Bank, however, means less power for old-line members from Europe. Will they go along? It seems unlikely unless the United States puts its weight behind Japan's request.

It remains for the United States to resolve its own ambivalence toward the congruence of burden sharing and power sharing with Japan. This is a tall order, and many issues, including Japan's military contribution to Western security and attendant issues like the thorny FSX fighter plane dispute, are involved.

Populism, Marxism, and Politics

If the Washington view of the third world debt problem is that Latin American populism and smoldering Marxism constitute a significant threat to hemispheric security, then Washington must decide whether it wishes to take a leading political and financial role in ensuring that security or whether it wishes to share the burden and, with it, some power and global prestige with Japan.

Messrs. Bush, Brady, and Baker will have to put their heads together and come up with a decision. They face more than the problems so far enumerated in designing a workable solution to the debt problem. They still need to grapple with the underlying economic aspects of the debt problem facing borrowers as well as lenders.

The fact that Washington has been responsive to the political tone of the third world debt does not change some stubborn economic realities. In a nutshell, the quality of third world debt as a financial asset valued in the marketplace has deteriorated sharply since 1987. Meanwhile, most American banks have reduced their exposure to these poorer quality loans but, as already explained, not in most cases by an amount proportional to the drop in the value of the loans.

The problem for the debtor countries that underlies the market's devaluation of their promises to pay is the same as it has been since the onset of the crisis stage in August 1982. The volume of loans contracted during the inflationary period before 1982 can be repaid only if inflation and with it the prices of goods and commodities, including oil, sold by debtor countries stay high or continue to rise. This has not happened: $20-a-barrel oil in 1989 is only $7-a-barrel oil in 1973, or pre-OPEC prices. The real burden of third world debt has been far above what was anticipated because while the prices of oil and other commodities have failed to rise as much as had been anticipated, interest rates have remained high because of the necessary initiatives in the 1980s in industrial countries to bring down inflation.

Since the spring of 1988 the effort under way in industrial countries to contain a resurgence of inflation has intensified the real economic pressures on debtor countries by raising their interest costs by more than can be compensated for by increases in commodity prices. The debtor countries are now no better off, and in some cases are worse off, than they were when the debt crisis appeared in 1982.

Table 2–1 shows the total external debt of fifteen debtor countries that accounts for the bulk of the third world debt. Since 1981 total external debt has risen by 45 percent (about 5.5 percent per year) from $348 billion to $505 billion. Interest payments on that debt have risen from 22 percent of exports to 26 percent of exports, meaning that over a quarter of foreign exchange earnings must go to service external debts.

Most of the increase in debt has been to official and nonbank creditors, including the IMF and the World Bank. Debts to official and nonbank lenders nearly doubled from $114 billion in 1981 to $220 billion at the end of 1988 while total debts to commercial banks rose by only 22 percent, from $234 billion in 1981 to $285 billion at the end of 1988.

The largest share of the $285 billion in debt to commercial banks was in long-term loans with the banks having converted over half of their short-term claims on developing-country debtors into long-term claims.

Debt Burden Intransigence

The result of such debt burden intransigence for the debtor countries has been a combination, with the mixture varying widely from country to country, of unwillingness or inability to pay interest or principal on debts. Argentina, the most desperate case among the major debtors, has not made regular interest payments on its $60 billion in external debt since April 1988. Inflation is running at an annual rate of over 400 percent, and the government may fall in May elections to opposition

TABLE 2–1

DEBT BURDEN OF FIFTEEN DEBTOR COUNTRIES, 1981 AND 1988
(billions of dollars and percent)

	End 1981	End 1988
Total external debt	348	505
Owed to commercial banks		
Long term	138	240
Short term	96	45
Owed to official and nonbank creditors	114	220
Total interest payments	36	42
Percentage of exports	22	26

NOTE: Argentina, Bolivia, Brazil, Chile, Colombia, Ecuador, Ivory Coast, Mexico, Morocco, Nigeria, Peru, Philippines, Uruguay, Venezuela, and Yugoslavia.
SOURCE: Morgan Guaranty Trust Co.

Peronists. Meanwhile, the market price for Argentina's debt has fallen from 62–65 cents per dollar in January 1987 to 16–17 cents per dollar in April 1989. (See table 2–2 for the market valuation of loans to major debtors.)

Venezuela's newly elected President Carlos Andres Perez also faces a very difficult situation that has been reflected in the market valuation of his nation's external debt. The government's cash reserves are below $1 billion against $3.5 billion in interest due in 1989 on its $35 billion external debt. While Venezuela's underlying economic situation is sounder than Argentina's—it has never borrowed from the IMF and could draw about $1.5 billion through its quota and a standby loan—its willingness to pay in the light of domestic political reality is in question. As a result of these and other uncertainties, the market value of its debt has dropped from 72–74 cents per dollar in January 1987 to about 35 cents per dollar in April 1989.

Brazil's usually booming economy has stagnated over the past year, and inflation has run close to 1,000 percent. Possible political gains by the Left in elections set for November 1989 have raised more concerns in the market about the value of Brazil's $120 billion in external debt. The market price of Brazilian debt dropped from about 75 cents per dollar in January 1987 to less than half that by January 1989 and has stayed at about 35 cents per dollar so far in 1989.

Mexico, heavily dependent on oil wealth and with some record of conforming to tough IMF prescriptions for adjustment, has managed to avoid further erosion in market valuation of its debt since 1988 year end. The market price of its debt dropped from about 55 cents per dollar

---

TABLE 2–2

MARKET VALUATION OF DEVELOPING-COUNTRY DEBT,
SELECTED DATES, 1985–1989
(as a percentage of book value)

Country	July 1985	Jan. 1986	Jan. 1987	Jan. 1988	Jan. 12 1989	Jan. 20 1989	Apr. 10 1989
Argentina	60-65	62-66	62-65	30-33	21-22	18-19	16-17
Brazil	75-81	75-81	74-76.5	44-47	38-40	34-35	34-35
Chile	65-69	65-69	65-68	60-63	58-60	60-61	58-59
Mexico	80-82	69-73	54-57	50-52	40-41	38-39	41-42
Peru	45-50	25-30	16-19	2-7	5-8	5-8	N.A.
Venezuela	81-83	80-82	72-74	55-57	38-39	37-38	35-36

N.A. = not available.
SOURCE: Shearson Lehman Hutton Inc. and Barron's.

in January 1987 to as low as 35 cents per dollar in March 1989. So far Mexico appears to have been the major beneficiary of the Brady initiative with the price of its debt having recovered to about 41 cents per dollar between March and April 1989.

Decline in the Market Price of Debt

With the market price of the debt of major Latin American borrowers on average cut in half in just two years since January 1987, it is clear that the banks that made the largest provisions for reserve losses and sold or swapped away as much of the developing-country debt as possible have made the soundest decisions when judged by market criteria. There is an awkward problem, however, that confronts any effort to write down loans—to forgive loans from the borrowers' perspective—in exchange for guarantees on the remaining, the unforgiven, portion. Banks that have made the least provision for loan losses are rewarded the most.

From 1987 to 1988 large American banks reduced their exposure to developing-country debt by about a third. (See table 2–3.) On average, thirteen of America's largest banks cut the ratio of such loans to shareholders' equity from 137 percent to about 100 percent through growth of equity and sales or swaps of that debt. While exposure was cut, the value of loans fell, too. What is the net effect on the financial position of a typical large bank of a combination of falling exposure to developing-country debt and a falling value of that debt from 1987 to 1988?

A typical large American bank, in round numbers, would have $100 billion in assets. Shareholders' equity would be about $4 billion for a gearing ratio of 25 to 1. An average 15 percent return on equity would yield annual earnings of about $600 million. At 100 percent of equity such a bank's exposure to developing-country debt would be $4 billion, based on the book value of the loan. The bank's problem is that the market value of the $4 billion in book value of developing-country debt is about 35 cents per dollar or $1.40 billion. The bank has lost $2.6 billion or over four years' earnings on these loans.

Such losses could be absorbed over ten years at a rate of $260 million per year. Discounting at 10 percent, the present value of $260 million per year in losses is $1.6 billion, a little less than one-third of the $5.12 billion present value of the bank's earnings over ten years, assuming that the earnings grow at the inflation rate so that discounting can be done at 3 percent.

In a comparison of the present value of loan losses discounted over ten years with the present value of growing earnings over ten years, the same calculation that today yields a ratio of about one-third, yielded a ratio of about one-fifth at the end of 1986. On the basis of this calcula-

17

TABLE 2–3
AMERICAN BANKS' EXPOSURE TO DEVELOPING-COUNTRY DEBT, 1987 AND 1988
(billions of dollars and percent)

	1987		1988	
	Loan portfolio	As % of equity	Loan portfolio	As % of equity
BankAmerica	7.8	263	7.1	200
Bank of Boston	0.8	44	0.4	20
Bankers Trust	3.0	133	3.0	94
Chase Manhattan	6.7	185	6.4	148
Chemical Bank	4.6	156	4.5	43
Citicorp	11.3	N.A.	9.5	N.A.
First Chicago	2.2	129	1.4	71
First Interstate	1.2	48	0.8	33
J. P. Morgan	4.1	86	3.6	7
Manufacturers Hanover	7.2	302	7.1	244
Republic New York	0.4	28	0.3	22
Security Pacific	1.3	48	0.8	21
Wells Fargo	1.1	55	0.9	36
Thirteen-bank composite	51.6	137	45.7	101

N.A. = not available.
SOURCE: Salomon Brothers.

tion alone, one could conclude that, overall, the banks' position has been harmed more by the loss in market value of developing-country debt than it has been helped by the reduction in their exposure to that debt.

To the extent that banks' loan-loss reserves have risen, they could have compensated for some of this deterioration. For example, between 1987 and 1988 if a given bank had increased its loan-loss reserves to $2.6 billion from about $1 billion, the increased negative impact of losses in market value of developing-country debt upon earnings would have been fully offset. While there have been some increases in loan-loss reserves by some banks since 1987, on average the increase has been small, and in some cases there have been decreases.

The banks, therefore, would seem to benefit from a settlement of the debt problem that guarantees on average a value of written-down debt over about one-third of its book value. A typical bank with $4 billion in loans carrying a current market value of about $1.4 billion would see the market value of its developing-country loans rise to $2.0 billion under a credible guarantee of such loans at 50 percent of book value. Its assets valued at market price (the basic determinant of the bank's stock price) would rise by $600 million, the equivalent of a full year's earnings. Spread over ten years, the $600 million is the approximate equivalent of a 10 percent rise in annual earnings that should result in a 10 percent rise in stock price and a lower cost of capital for the bank.

The Last Shall Be First

A problem for the banks with offering guarantees on the remainder of written-down developing-country loans lies with the "last shall be first" phenomenon. Suppose a typical bank had been more reckless and instead of holding $4 billion in developing-country debt held $8 billion with all else the same so that this debt made up 200 percent of shareholders' equity. At 35 percent of book value those debt holdings would have a market value of $2.8 billion. With a 50 percent guarantee, market value would rise by $1.2 billion to $4 billion. The gain for the less prudent bank is twice that for the prudent bank. In general, gains rise proportionately with exposure to such debt. The market value guarantee scheme would mean that the last shall be first among banks managing exposure to developing-country debt. The share prices of "the last" would rise relative to the share prices of "the first." The strategy of waiting for a public sector bailout would be rewarded over the strategy of actively managing exposure to the debt, a perverse reward structure that would discourage sound management in the banking sector.

Some compensation scheme to see that rewards of the write-down strategy are more equitably distributed will have to be devised before the banks will agree to any such scheme among themselves, let alone agree with debtor countries, governments, and international institutions. It may be necessary to pool the gains and distribute them to banks as guaranteed claims on a debt-management facility in a way that produces at least equal percentage gains in earnings for all banks so that relative stock prices are left unaffected by the settlement.

Conclusion

A solution to the debt problem that incorporates forgiveness or write-downs that the Brady approach contemplates will have to be structured to reward virtuous performance in borrowing countries and lending banks. The proportional reward scheme that leaves the relative prices of bank shares unaffected would have to be coupled with a scheme that avoids the moral hazard problem. That is, borrowing countries must not be rewarded with larger forgiveness if unsound policies have driven down the market value of their debts relative to the market value of debts of countries like Chile that have been more soundly managed. The latter problem could be addressed by requiring higher interest rates on debts of countries whose liabilities are valued less by the market. Debt-service relief could be earned by structural reforms prescribed by the debt facility that are in turn recognized by market participants as enhancing the value of previously devalued debt.

Whatever the outcome, the Brady proposal will become just another vain hope unless the legitimate concerns of borrowers and lenders are recognized in the design of an actual plan to deal with the debt problem. The primary aim of such a plan must be to reward past and prospective sound adjustment behavior by both lending banks and borrowing countries. Failing that, any plan will founder on the shoals of disagreements among and between borrowers and lenders.

3

Reducing Transfers from Debtor Countries

Rudiger Dornbusch

Over the past seven years a muddling through strategy on the debt of developing countries helped improve bank balance sheets. Whatever the wisdom of that strategy, there is little doubt that it extracted an awesome price in debtor countries. While banks are in a much better position to face debt reduction, many debtor countries have experienced an economic and social setback, if not destruction. The need for reconstruction is apparent from the dramatic deterioration in the Latin American standard of living. Figure 3–1 shows the decline and stagnation of income per head in the 1980s. These data, however, are favorably influenced by the Brazilian experience of moderate positive growth.

The Brady plan for debt reduction recognizes the urgent need, political and economic, to get to work on reconstruction in Latin America. The change in strategy is late, welcome, and inadequate. It imposes little structure on the debt-service adjustments to be accomplished. In that way it may enhance the costs to banks and debtor countries of the debt impasse.

Treasury Secretary Nicholas Brady has started an avalanche, impossible to reverse and, in the best of conditions, difficult to control. Under the Brady plan banks hope to get major guarantees (at little cost) for their increasingly poor Latin American loans; debtor countries see the Brady plan as a response to their longstanding demand to write debts down to the secondary market price.

The gulf can be bridged to both parties' satisfaction only if public money from the International Monetary Fund (IMF) and the World Bank is hijacked for the purpose. Without public guarantees on the required scale, two possibilities emerge: either banks are forced, by regulatory requirements, to pass on to debtors relief at the expense of their stockholders, or else banks are left untouched and debtors go without

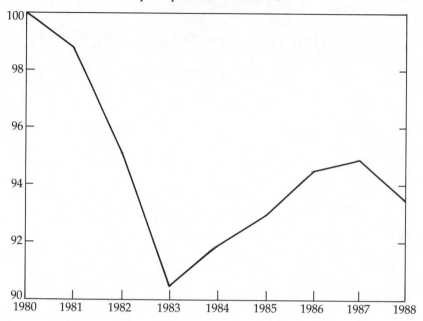

FIGURE 3–1
LATIN AMERICA'S PER CAPITA REAL INCOME, 1980–1988
(per capita, index 1980=100)

SOURCE: UN Economic Commission for Latin America.

much relief. In that event, no doubt, self-administered relief will become the rule.

This chapter reviews the key problem of resource transfers and evaluates alternative strategies of debt-service reduction. The unifying conceptual scheme is the transfer problem in its *fiscal* and in its *dollar* aspects. Before we go to the transfer problem, we briefly note a central fact: since 1982 the muddling through strategy has deteriorated both debt and the ability for debt service (see table 3–1). Debt ratios are far higher today than they were in 1982, and that point is, of course, recognized in the secondary market.

The market also recognizes, however, that the value of debt is impaired not only by the accrued debt overhang. It is also impaired by the erosion of a political will or even by legitimacy of debt service.

The Transfer Problem and Debt-Service Fatigue

Why is debt service such a problem?[1] In one sense the answer is quite straightforward: countries that used to spend, borrowing the resources

TABLE 3-1

EXTERNAL DEBT AS PERCENTAGE OF GROSS DOMESTIC PRODUCT
FOR LATIN AMERICA AND SEVENTEEN INDEBTED COUNTRIES,
SELECTED YEARS, 1980–1987

	1980	1982	1987
Latin America	35.3	46.3	60.1
Seventeen indebted countries[a]	32.8	45.0	63.1

a. Seventeen highly indebted countries identified by the World Bank.
SOURCE: World Bank, *World Debt Tables* 1988–1989.

from official and private creditors (with little thought of how to service or even less repay the loans), now no longer command these resources: they are limited to spending even less than the value of domestic production. The adjustment is complicated by two facts. The first is the macroeconomics of earning foreign exchange; the second is the political economy problem of finding extra budget resources for debt service. These issues are familiar from the German experience of reparation payments following World War I. Exactly the same issues arise in the context of the involuntary debt service now under way.

The Reduction in Spending. The first issue is how a country adjusts to a reduction in its spendable resources. Before the debt crisis foreign loans supplemented domestic income, enlarging the resources that could be spent. Interest payments on loans were automatically provided in the form of new money, and the principal on debts was automatically rolled over. With management of the debt so easy, and with ready access to resources beyond what was required to service the debt, spending ran high. After credit rationing began in 1982, spending had to be limited, and absorption fell below the level of output as interest now had to be paid out of current production. Interest payments now had to be earned by noninterest surpluses in the current account.

Table 3-2 shows the debt-service process at work. In the post-1982 period of involuntary lending, debtor countries have achieved a shift in their noninterest external balance of nearly 5 percent of gross domestic product (GDP). This improvement in the external balance serves to make net transfers of interest to the creditors. It is matched by a nearly equal reduction in investment in the debtor countries.

This perverse transfer of resources, of course, comes at the expense of living standards in the developing countries. More important,

TABLE 3–2

ECONOMIC GROWTH, INFLATION, INVESTMENT, AND TRANSFER
OF INTEREST IN LATIN AMERICA, 1970–1988
(percent)

	1970–1980	1980–1988
Growth	3.1	-0.8
Inflation	36.7	123.0
Investment (as percentage of GDP)	23.5	18.7
Transfer (as percentage of GDP)[a]	-2.6	3.5

a. 1973–1981 and 1982–1988 respectively.
SOURCE: IMF and UN Economic Commission for Latin America.

though, the transfer has as a counterpart a sharp decline in investment. Interest payments are thus really financed by a mortgage on future standards of living and on the debtors' growth potential. In countries where population growth is high and income distribution is radically unbalanced, such a policy may turn out to be very shortsighted.

The issue of how to distribute the cut in spending between its various components—government, consumption, and investment—however, remained. As we saw above, a large part of the cut took the form of reduced investment. There was, of course, also a decline in consumption, however. Because of two special features of the adjustment process, a fall in investment was not enough. First, cutting total demand has macroeconomic multiplier effects that translate into a reduction in output, income, and hence private spending. Second, at the same time that involuntary debt service started, a deterioration in the world economy also occurred that required an extra downward adjustment in spending.

The Foreign Exchange Problem. The second macroeconomic issue in adjusting to debt concerns Latin America's need to earn dollars, not pesos. In the 1970s debtors were borrowing abroad, supplementing domestic incomes with foreign resources. Since 1982 they have been forced to make large outward transfers (see figure 3–2). These transfers require a trade surplus. The cut in spending will, of course, reduce import demand and also free exportables for sale abroad, but for two reasons that will not be enough. First, a sizable fraction of the expenditure cut will fall on domestic (nontraded) goods, not tradables. The spending cut thus directly creates unemployment rather than potential foreign exchange earnings. Even for those goods that are directly tradable, it is not necessarily the case that increased supplies can be

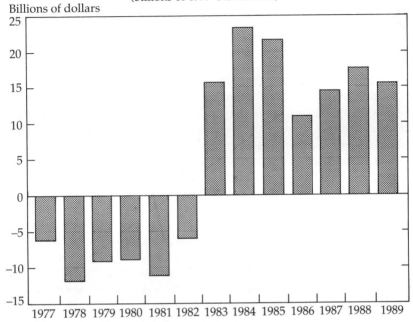

FIGURE 3–2
LATIN AMERICA'S EXTERNAL TRANSFER OF RESOURCES, 1977–1989
(billions of 1977 U.S. dollars)

SOURCE: UN Economic Commission for Latin America.

sold. Often obtaining market access is a problem, and, if the goods are not homogeneous commodities like cotton or copper, a cut in their price is required to realize increased sales. Even then, unless demand is sufficiently responsive, total earnings may not increase.

Translating the spending cut into foreign exchange earnings requires a gain in competitiveness. The gain in competitiveness draws resources into the tradable-goods sector and in the world market makes it possible to sell the increased production of tradable goods. Of course, the only way to gain competitiveness is by reducing the wage in dollars by a real depreciation. At least in the short run, however, the real wage cut also generates increased unemployment as the spendable income of workers is cut. The size of the required cut in real wages deserves further comment. It is larger the larger the share of tradable goods in income and the smaller the share of wages in GDP.

The overwhelming difficulty in the adjustment process is that external adjustment via a gain in competitiveness reduces employment. The dominant effect on employment is from the reduction in real wages and the resulting reduction in domestic demand. The positive employment response that would be expected in the tradable-goods sector

25

from the gain in competitiveness is often very weak and slow, partly because expectations of a *sustained* change in competitiveness do not take hold immediately. The traded-goods sector thus adopts a wait-and-see attitude, which makes real depreciation a highly precarious policy tool. The Mexican experience in this respect is particularly instructive.

A second important difficulty arises from the worldwide adjustment to forced debt service. Since most debtor countries were overspending in the early 1980s and are now under a forced debt-service regime, they all had to resort to real depreciation to enhance their competitiveness. That means they are competitively cutting their wages relative to each other, however, and not only relative to those of the creditor countries. As a result, an isolated country, cutting its dollar wage, say, by 50 percent, will gain much less in increased dollar revenues because all the competing developing countries are doing much the same.

The Budget Problem. The third macroeconomic problem in the adjustment process involves the budget. Much of the external debt is public or publicly guaranteed. Of the part that was not initially in the public sector, much has wound up there in the aftermath of the crises, as a result of bank failures. The government thus winds up having to service a debt that before was either in private hands or automatically serviced by new money. The problem, of course, is where to find the extra 3 or 4 percent of budget revenue that will pay these new interest costs.

There are basically four avenues: raising taxes and public sector prices, reducing government outlays, printing money, or issuing domestic debt. Raising taxes is notoriously difficult since most of the taxes are already levied in the form of social security taxes on workers. An easier solution is to raise public sector prices or to eliminate subsidies. The elimination of subsidies is particularly cheered by creditors and international agencies since it means moving closer to efficient resource allocation.[2] Of course, the imposition of extra taxes or the withdrawal of subsidies inevitably causes prices to inflate unless the tax increase or subsidy cut is offset by a reduction in other prices or wages. Of course, budget cutting via the revenue side reduces the growth in money, and hence, in combination, it leads to a recession with inflationary pressure sustained by prevailing inflation.

Cutting government spending is another option. Attention here focuses on the often extreme inefficiency of the public sector. The public perceives that there must be a way to pay the bills out of increased efficiency, rather than reduced private absorption. The fact is, of course, that there is very little room for public sector improvements in the short term. Large-scale firing of redundant workers would create an overwhelming political problem. Plant closings are of the same kind, and selling inefficient, overunionized firms runs into the obvious problem that the potential buyers might need to be paid to take over the liability. Perhaps the best advice may be that public sector firms should be simply given away. The problem is that the workers might oppose even that.

The most common adjustment is a cut in or freeze of public sector wages. This has happened in most of the debtor countries, in some cases on a very large scale. Although it does help the budget, it presents its own problems. The reduction in relative wages for the public sector promotes an exodus of the wrong kind: efficient workers leave, and only those with little alternative stay.

In many of the debtor countries the answer to forced debt service has almost inevitably been to increase government budget deficits and to finance this by issuing debt or by printing money. Money finance brings with it the problem of high—often extreme—inflation. It is no accident that Argentina and Brazil experienced extraordinary inflation rates in the aftermath of the debt crisis. When deficits are financed by debt, while the imminent inflation problem may be absent, excessive debt accumulation, which ultimately poses the risk of an inflationary liquidation or a repudiation, still remains an issue.

The foreign exchange problem interacts with the budget problem. The need to devalue to gain competitiveness implies that the value of debt service in the home currency increases. A given payment of, say, $1 billion now amounts to more in pesos, produces a larger peso deficit, and hence gives rise to the need for increased inflationary finance. Thus devaluation is a source of inflation not just directly by increasing the prices of traded goods and any accompanying indexation effects but also indirectly by raising the required inflation tax. In the classical hyperinflations major movements in the exchange rate were the prelude to the outbreak of uncontrolled inflation, and some evidence suggests that exactly the same process is at work in the debtor countries today.

The budget is also adversely affected by the problem of capital flight. To stem capital flight provoked by the inflationary consequences of debt service or perhaps by an impending tax reform, the country will have to raise real interest rates to very high levels. These high real interest rates in turn apply to the domestic debt, causing it to grow more rapidly and thereby raising future budget deficits and the prospect of instability. That in turn feeds more capital flight and yet higher rates. An extraordinary vicious circle thus surrounds the sudden need to service debt and the inability to do so through ordinary taxation.

It is worth recognizing an important trade-off in the adjustment process. To earn foreign exchange, a country must cut the real wage for

27

tradable goods, thus enhancing competitiveness. To balance the budget, however, that country must often cut subsidies for such items as food or transportation, and that action also means a cut in real wages. There is thus competition between two targets, a cut in the dollar wage or a cut in the tortilla wage. A choice must be made because one can cut only so much. The lags with which the trade sector adjusts suggest that the competitiveness adjustment should take precedence and that budget balancing should follow once the economy's resources are real-located. Since the real depreciation by itself is already bound to produce slack, overheating in this sequence of adjustment poses no risk.

A final notable point is the link between budget cutting and the extraordinary fall in Latin American investment. The reason is that in government spending the easiest cuts are in investment. Postponing investment and maintenance is much easier than firing workers. The resulting impact on aggregate investment is so large because the public sector, in the form of public sector enterprises, accounts for a great part of total investment and because the public sector has been in the fore-front of adjustment. It is immediately obvious that cutting spending on public enterprises is a very ineffective means of adjustment, failing to recognize the distinction between the public sector's current and capital accounts.

The Special Role of Capital Flight. A special complication of debt service arises with the flight of private capital (see table 3–3). Uncertainty about the exchange rate, or near-certainty about a forthcoming devaluation required to generate a trade surplus, will bring about an exodus of private capital. Thus in addition to debt service countries need resources to pay for the flight of private capital. Even with stringent capital controls, the net is not tight, and under- or overinvoicing of trade flows provides a ready escape. In many countries, however, capital controls are not even feasible or advisable, and hence the re-straints on capital movements are very small.

Investors have an option to postpone the return of capital, and they will wait until the frontloading of returns is sufficient to compensate for the risk of relinquishing the liquidity option of a wait-and-see position. This is the case even when interest rates are high and rewarding. Moreover, when capital does return, it chooses a highly liquid form, sitting, so to speak, in the parking lot (or on the tarmac), with the engine running. There is definitely little commitment to a rapid resumption of real investment because of residual uncertainty about whether stabilization can in fact be sustained.

How then can governments reassure investors? The common an-swer is to bring about a "credible" stabilization. In practice it comes

TABLE 3–3

ESTIMATES OF CAPITAL FLIGHT FOR
SIX LATIN AMERICAN COUNTRIES, 1976–1987
(cumulative without imputed interest, $U.S. billions)

	1976–1982	1983–1987	1976–1987 Total	Per Capita ($U.S.)
Argentina	22.4	6.7	29.1	924
Brazil	5.8	14.6	20.4	144
Mexico	25.3	35.3	60.6	745
Peru	N.A.	3.3	N.A.	N.A.
Philippines	4.5	1.1	5.6	98
Venezuela	20.7	19.4	40.1	2,195

N.A.= not available.
NOTE: These estimates use the World Bank method.
SOURCE: Don Lessard and John Williamson, eds., *Capital Flight and Third World Debt* (Washington, D.C.: Institute for International Economics, 1987); updated by the author.

down to high interest rates and a real exchange rate so competitive that expected further real depreciation is unlikely. High interest rates though are counterproductive from a point of view of growth because they lead to holding of paper assets rather than real investment. A low real exchange rate cuts the standard of living and thus reduces domestic demand and profitability for all investments except in the traded goods sector.

If real depreciation is not sufficient to bring about investment, however, the government faces a very awkward position: income is being redistributed from labor to capital, but because the real depreciation is not sufficient, the increased profits are taken out as flight capital. Labor will obviously insist then that the policy be reversed. This uncertainty is an important feature in understanding the relationship between real exchange rates and capital flight and the poststabilization difficulties in developing countries.

The capital flight problem can be thought of like a bank run: if the public is concerned about the value of its assets, it stages a run on the central bank and forces depreciation. The belief that everybody else will do the same reinforces each individual investor's belief that he must move out of domestic assets because the general exodus will, inevitably, force depreciation—hence the "run." The income distribution problems associated with capital flight, whether through slow growth,

TABLE 3–4

Problem Debtors in Latin America, the Philippines,
and Seventeen Countries, 1988
(billions of $U.S. and percent)

	Total Debt	Private	U.S. Banks	Nine Banks	Price (c/$)	Debt/GDP (percent)
Latin America	408.8	308.8	65.4	45.5	30.2	60. 1
Argentina	59.6	47.3	8.2	6.2	17.6	73. 9
Brazil	120.1	92.2	18.9	14.4	27.1	39.4
Chile	20.8	15.5	5.4	3.9	55.6	124.1
Colombia	17.2	8.3	2.2	1.4	50.5	50. 2
Mexico	107.4	83.8	19.3	12.2	33.4	77. 5
Venezuela	35.0	34.8	14.3	5.6	27.6	94.5
Philippines	30.2	18.2	4.2	3.0	36.5	86.5
Seventeen Countries[a]	528.6	377.9	69.1	50.9	-	63.1

a. Seventeen highly indebted countries identified by the World Bank.
Source: Federal Financial Institutions Examination Council, World Bank,
and Salomon Brothers.

high real interest rates, or real wage cutting, vastly increase the debt
problem.

The Quality of Debts

We noted above that debt ratios have been deteriorating over the
muddling through period. Here, we briefly present the deterioration of
debt.

TABLE 3–5

U.S. Bank Exposure in Latin America, 1985 and 1988
(billions of $U.S. and percent of capital)

	1985		1988[a]	
	Exposure	Percent[b]	Exposure	Percent[b]
All banks	80.4	78.9	65.4	48.1
Nine money banks	60.5	148.6	45.5	83.9

a. September 1988.
b. Exposure as percent of capital.
Source: Federal Financial Institutions Examination Council.

Table 3–4 shows the debt characteristics for the main debtor countries affected by the Baker plan.[3] One striking fact is that U.S. banks own only 15 percent of Latin America's total external debt. This small share reflects not only the presence of public debts in the total but also the major participation of Japan and Europe as lenders. Of total private claims on problem debtors, U.S. banks hold only 18 percent.

In the banks' balance sheet the debts of developing countries have clearly declined significantly since 1982. In that respect at least the muddling through strategy has been successful. In 1982 the money center banks could not have withstood a significant debt write-off. Today debt reduction is clearly digestible as table 3–5 shows.

One interesting feature of table 3–5 is the reduction in the face value of debt that has taken place since 1985. While the improvement of balance sheets has been attributable to raising capital and reserves, a $15 billion reduction in claims was also achieved through various kinds of swaps and buybacks.

Debt-Reduction Strategies

There are two central questions about debt reduction: all things considered, which is the best way to go about debt reduction, and how much debt reduction is necessary? Neither question will get a unanimous answer.[4]

The Debt Overhang. The question of the debt overhang is perhaps hardest to address. A country's public debt-service ability depends critically on the quality of its fiscal system. If the tax base is narrow and taxation is inefficient, the scope for debt service is exceptionally limited. High external debt means either an explosion of internal debt, as countries finance interest payments abroad by borrowing at home, or inflationary finance, perhaps reaching even hyperinflation, and an unjustifiable postponement of infrastructure investment in physical capital, education, and health.

In the short run a debtor country can easily face up to an excessive debt because these alternative options of budget adjustment or financing provide some leeway. Within a few years, however, it becomes clear that these are not realistic options. Moreover, if they are pursued too long or too vigorously, they add their own difficulties via capital flight or political deterioration.

By historical and international standards even the debts of Mexico or Brazil are not record highs: British debt in the nineteenth century exceeded 200 percent of GDP, and the debt ratio of Ireland or Israel today exceeds those in Latin America. Even these countries, however, although they have access to the world capital market, have extreme and possibly unsustainable fiscal difficulties. It is not clear what made the British nineteenth-century debt sustainable, but it is certain that sustainability of the public debts (internal plus external) in Brazil, Mexico, or Chile—to name only three—is in question. In Mexico it is especially clear that the budget balancing has come at the price of an unsustainable rollback of public sector investment. If growth is to resume, public sector infrastructure investment will be necessary, and that in combination with debt service is incompatible with budget balancing.

In the past seven years, according to World Bank data, the debt-to-GDP ratio of highly indebted countries has increased dramatically. On the current course of the world economy, a further deterioration is altogether likely.[5] Therefore *some* debt reduction is immediately appropriate. Unfortunately, there is no clearly defined threshold of unsustainability: in large measure the threshold will depend on growth rates of real income, real interest rates, and expectations about the terms of trade. In an optimistic scenario for the world economy a debt ratio (again, internal plus external) of 80 percent might be sustainable. With slow growth and high real interest rates in world markets, however, even that is incompatible with financial stability.

At this point we have no way of predicting which scenario will prevail. It therefore seems appropriate to make debt reduction *conditional* or, better yet, to link debt-service requirements directly to the external environment and growth performance of the debtors. Specifically, a scheme of debt reduction might involve first a removal of 50 percent of the debt and then an interest rate on the remainder positively linked to the country's growth rate.

A very significant difficulty in deciding on immediate, large debt reduction arises from the fact that the debt-service problem reflects not a physical inability to service debts but rather a combination of mismanagement, unwillingness, and political complications. A major fiscal reform that achieves a broad and comprehensive tax base, specifically including middle- and upper-income groups, is an essential counterpart of debt reduction. There is little or no excuse for the low yields from taxation in debtor countries. Debt reduction should therefore be conditioned on far-reaching fiscal reform.

A further difficulty arises in deciding how much of the debt reduction should fall on internal as opposed to external debt. To a large extent these debt reductions are substitutable. Domestic debt reduction should certainly be contemplated as part of a major restructuring of debt and public finance.

Another point concerns external debt owed to official creditors. In the discussion on debt reduction (except in Africa) the attention focuses on private debt and rarely on public debt. There is little justification for singling out private creditors alone for debt reduction.

A final consideration is how to treat the sizable flight of capital abroad. Under favorable conditions this clearly represents a partial, and in some countries major, offset against debt. The difficulty is that this capital would return only under favorable conditions, which means with major debt relief. Thus stopping capital flight requires debt relief, but if that capital does return, less debt reduction is required. To get around this special conundrum, the proposal to recycle interest deserves special attention.

In summary, we have no answer to the debt overhang problem. When the debt ratios are rapidly rising without a clear prospect of reversal, obviously an overhang exists. Solutions involve two adjustments: a broader-based and more efficient taxation and public administration and a reduction in debt service. Both will contain the buildup of debt and the resulting excess debt that stems from capital flight. The distribution between the two adjustments is largely a political decision and a bargaining issue.

We next turn to the chief vehicles for debt reduction.

Swaps. Debt-equity swaps and debt-debt swaps need little comment. It is by now well established that they rarely serve the interests of the creditor. The reasons include the following four considerations:

• Conversions rarely present *additional* resources; conversions frequently apply to projects that would have taken place even without a discount. As a result, the Central Bank loses foreign exchange that could have been used for debt reduction or other priority assignments.

• Conversions have to be financed. A country in debt difficulties typically faces far higher borrowing costs on new debt than on captive debt. As a result, the implied refinancing raises the debt-service cost dramatically.

• Conversions, because they convey the right to remit earnings and principal within a few years, liquefy the external debt. With a conversion a debtor loses the ability to control the outflow of foreign exchange and thus becomes more vulnerable.

• Conversions are a one-way street. If resources are committed, because of credit rationing, they are lost irretrievably.

These arguments against debt swaps have been accepted in the aftermath of a few years of bad experience. The extravagant, unjustifiable Brazilian excesses in swapping everything that moved have no doubt been the chief piece of evidence. Other countries had already recognized earlier that their interests were poorly served by swaps.

The Chilean case remains the exception, chiefly because domestic interest rates were not far higher than in New York so that a refinancing, capturing part of the discount, could be profitable. Even in

Chile, though, the liquefaction of the external debt will present a major difficulty for the democratic government.

Buybacks. The development of the secondary market, just as in the 1940s, has created an active interest in debt buybacks as a means of debt reduction. In the 1940s debt repatriation was an important part of the reduction of external debt. Specifically, Chile reduced its external debt in the mid-1930s by one-third, using $13 million to repurchase $88 million, thus paying on average fifteen cents on the dollar.

The first major initiative on buybacks occurred in the Mexico-Morgan deal. The results of this deal were disappointing because the cash component in the form of a zero-coupon bond represented only a small fraction of the new instrument, leaving the chief portion in interest payments without well-established seniority. Another buyback, by Bolivia, achieved significant debt reduction. Even that operation, however, has been questioned. The issue, hotly debated, is whether debt reduction is a good idea for a debtor country. The question involves the alternative use of the resources committed to the buyback. It is not enough to argue that a buyback is interesting because of the discount: there is a discount because some creditors believe that the competing uses of resources will take priority over debt service.

The case against debt buybacks has been made most forcefully by Jeremy Bulow and Kenneth Rogoff.[6] Their position, put simply, is this: debtor countries cannot gain when they make bad states worse by using scarce resources for debt reduction. The only advantage of debt reduction occurs in good states. With a reduction in the face value of debt, the debtor country gains a larger share of that good state—what is left over after creditors have taken what they can up to full debt service. The more effective creditors are in collecting when countries can pay, the more interest a country has in reducing the face value of debt. This can occur only in bad states, however, when resources have highly profitable alternative uses. Hence the cost-benefit analysis of a buyback involves the trade-off between good and bad states, between the discount and the extent to which creditors can enforce their claims in good states.

They argue that if creditors in good states can collect only relatively little and if conversion takes place at modest discounts, using resources with alternative uses, buybacks amount to throwing money in the wind. Put in this way, countries and markets may clearly have become mesmerized by the discounts and engaged in impulse buying rather than in reasoned cost-benefit analysis.

The Bulow-Rogoff presumption, while pointing to an important consideration, oversimplifies and possibly misses critical aspects of the issue. Let us now consider a classification that brings into the discussion two important features of debt conversion and buybacks. The essential criteria are whether extra resources (strictly additional and earmarked) are made available by the rest of the world for the operation or whether a country has to use its own resources (reserves or trade surpluses). The other dimension concerns gains from a reduction in the face value of debt, which are here referred to as efficiency gains. They include the beneficial effects on investment of debt reduction (and hence increased profitability of private industry via lower taxes in good states), reduced financial instability, and the accompanying reduction in capital flight. A reduction in the face value of debt may or may not bring about a broad range of these benefits.

It is clear that when extra *earmarked* resources become available and can be used for debt reduction with potentially large efficiency gains, a debtor should go ahead. The same remains true if the efficiency gains are negligible. Without extra resources and without gains in extra efficiency, however, countries would undoubtedly misallocate resources and priorities in practicing debt reduction. This leaves only the interesting case where there are no extra resources but where some efficiency gains can be expected. Here the Bulow-Rogoff cost-benefit analysis must be applied. If the efficiency gains are small (creditors cannot capture much of the extra income in a good state), then a country is better off investing than reducing the face value of its debt. This is the case Bulow and Rogoff argue holds empirically.

Others have argued that these efficiency gains may be very large because they include gains in macroeconomic stability, including sharply reduced capital flight. Of course, it is also possible that the cost of making resources available for debt buybacks is very large. This is certainly the case when, as in Brazil today, inflationary finance is used for informal debt conversions. In that case buybacks may be a source of increased rather than reduced financial instability and capital flight. Another fact that points in this direction is that buybacks are a one-way street when a country is credit constrained. Using reserves, as Mexico did to retire debt, seemed a good idea at the time because reserves were plentiful. Less than six months later, however, the country was on the verge of a major devaluation because it did not have the reserves to support the exchange rate and yet did not want to face the confrontation of a stop on debt service. Bankers were pleased that they had taken the money then; they certainly will not give it back. Mexico would have done better to have held on to its reserves, a point many observers made at the time. The situation is not always as obvious as it was in Mexico's case, however. Unfortunately, without a simple and sturdy test of the importance of these efficiency gains, the argument must remain open.

Beyond the efficiency gains already noted, we must also consider the implications of buybacks for creditor-debtor relations. Buybacks may be a means to avoid conflict. It is not apparent what creditors could and would be willing to do to enforce their claims. Perhaps they could do very little, and hence (morality aside) it is surprising that debtors do service at least part of their debt. It is also possible, though, that, particularly in the event of frivolous nonservice, creditors would receive political support to inflict major damage on unwilling debtors. This uncertainty about the consequences of partial or full default are a burden on the economic prospects of debtor economies. Cooperation in debt-reduction schemes may be the price to pay for reduced debt service without penalty. It may simply be a "check-is-in-the-mail strategy," which, practiced on a modest scale, avoids the necessity of keeping interest payments current on the entire debt. As long as outright nonpayment is a taboo, buybacks may be a relatively cheap rescheduling strategy. Of course, when countries pay *all* the interest as Mexico did and Brazil expects to do, this argument does not hold.

A successful opportunity for buybacks almost seems a contradiction in terms: if debtors do have the money, the discount will be small and uninteresting. If they do not have the money, the discount will be large but beyond reach. An important opportunity remains, however, that arises from the contamination factor: today *all* Latin American debt trades at a discount, even the debt of Colombia—notwithstanding the fact that this country has continuously serviced its debt in respect to interest and principal. If capital markets do not discriminate between debtors, relatively well-performing debtors have an opening to buy out particularly ill-informed (or constrained) creditors. Colombia, whose debt trades at a 50 percent discount, faces an overriding temptation to use its resources for buybacks rather than amortization. An even better use of the resources might be domestic investment financed by forced lending on the part of creditors.

For those debtors who face an acute liquidity shortage, Mexico, for example, the very limited resources rather than being dissipated in buybacks can be more effectively used to promote domestic financial stability, imports, and growth. One means of doing so is to use budget resources to service debt in local currency, allowing creditors to use them for unrestricted investment but not for repatriation. Rather than making transfers abroad, the debtor would experience investment and growth. In a second phase, just as after World War II, there might be a cleaning out of debts, prior to a return to the world capital market. At that time Mexico settled at twenty cents on the dollar, and other Latin American countries, with the exception of Argentina, which retired debt at par, all achieved major debt reduction. By historical standards, then, it is much too early to buy out the creditors. Ten years from now they may be eager to settle at ten or twenty cents on the dollar. For debtor countries, however, holding out is also costly; the unresolved debt overhang can be a source of capital flight and macroeconomic instability. An early, even if less drastic, debt reduction is, therefore, preferable.

Interest Reduction or Buybacks? In the context of the Brady plan, it is useful to ask whether resources should be concentrated on reduction of principal or of interest. Although both contribute to a reduction of debt service, they operate quite differently. Granted in exchange for guarantees, interest reductions, rolling one year at a time, maximize the leverage of a given pool of debt-relief resources. Exit bonds paid in full are at the other extreme in that they maximize the use of scarce resources. They do so directly because debt is immediately paid off, albeit at a discount, but also because it is likely that secondary market prices will rise in anticipation of a cash offer, as indeed they already have.[7]

A carefully designed buyback scheme should seek rolling interest reduction in preference to reduction of face value. There is some scope to combine zero-coupon bonds with rolling guarantees, which may facilitate regulatory problems for banks. A strong presumption exists against exit bonds or major buybacks at the market price.

Interest Recycling

Much of the discussion on debt reduction does not distinguish sufficiently between the two sources of debt difficulties: one is the budget problem; the other is the dollar or the trade problem. It is not necessarily the case that countries experience *equally* or at all the two problems. It is perfectly conceivable that one country has a budget problem but no trade problem; the other country has a trade surplus and thus from a foreign exchange point of view is in a position to service debt, while its fiscal situation is not sufficiently solid to entertain debt service.

When external transfer problems predominate, the problem can be addressed not only by debt-service reduction but also by a fundamental restructuring of debt service in a manner that takes care of the major part of interest payments due. Actual payments in dollars would be reduced to the service of trade credit and the loans of multilateral organizations. A large share of the remaining interest payments would in part be capitalized, thus freeing resources for much-needed public sector investment, and in part they would be made in local currency. Creditors who receive the local currency payments could use them for unrestricted investment in the debtor countries' economies. The only limitation on the use of funds would be that they could not be transferred abroad. The claims to these payments could, however, be sold.

To clarify the issue, consider the cases of Brazil and Mexico in 1988. Brazil had a current account surplus of $4 billion; clearly there was no foreign exchange problem. Brazil did have a major budget deficit, however, at least 4 percent of GDP in official estimates but quite possibly as much 7 percent. In Brazil's case the problem is clearly that the budget transfer, not the external transfer, is the issue. Debt reduction would help (either domestic or external), and fiscal and public administration reform would do the same.

In Mexico's case the external balance is the problem; the budget, including real interest payments, is only in a moderate deficit, but the current account shows a deficit of more than $6 billion. In this situation interest recycling offers a possibility of avoiding extra strain from the dollar shortage.

Colombia offers another example where recycling would be useful. The budget deficit and the current account show moderate deficits. The external balance constraint is an obstacle to higher growth and higher investment. Under recycling, resources could be diverted from a trade surplus to domestic investment. Colombia's problems are in no way extreme. In fact, the country has met debt service continuously and has been able to do so under conditions of sustained growth and moderate inflation. The difficulty, solved by recycling, is that capital markets are unwilling to provide new money simply because of Latin American contamination. Unilateral recycling, combined with some capitalization for the public sector, seems an appropriate response to this kind of market failure.

Argentina is a fourth case: here we have a large current-account deficit and a large budget deficit. Nothing short of a dramatic reduction of debt service, combined with serious public sector reform, can restore stability.

Favorable Features of Recycling. There are several advantages of interest recycling:

• The transfer of resources abroad is suspended. Rather than running trade surpluses, debtor countries have resources freed that can be devoted to investment. Of course, serious budget action is required to ensure that in fact the resources go into investment rather than consumption. The shift of resources toward investment has two effects. It implies an expansion in capacity and thus sustains job creation. This issue is central in an economy where labor force growth rates above 3 percent have created major imbalances between labor supply and demand. The expansion in capacity removes the bottlenecks that today stand in the way of growth. Growth, in turn, translates into more stable public finance via a broadened tax base.

• The scheme creates a more stable and prosperous business environment. With the current strategy a foreign exchange bottleneck is always around the corner, and the reaction is invariably a contraction of demand and a depreciation of exchange. This reality has led to a lack of interest in productive investment and to extensive capital flight. The center of gravity has shifted to financial markets, far away from productive activity. By removing the need for immediate debt service, the debtor economy can resume a more balanced position with an emphasis on long-term investment and growth. As a lever for reversing capital flight, there is no better way than a restoration of business confidence and an end of exchange pressure. Recycling also offers two further advantages to creditor countries: it avoids outright debt relief (or debt default) and hence avoids large-scale involvement of the taxpayers of the creditor country. Furthermore, by providing debtors with room for growth, recycling affords every expectation of increased exports to debtor countries and a reduction in the currently high levels of imports.

• There is a third, once-and-for-all gain. In the present situation the need to maintain very depreciated real exchange rates translates into inflationary pressures and low demand in the debtors' domestic markets. The removal of external constraints allows some real appreciation and hence provides a breathing space for stabilization of inflation. Inflation stabilization is, of course, an essential quid pro quo in a restoration of normal business conditions.

• Interest recycling, by removing exchange rate uncertainty, creates an essential precondition for a return of capital.

• Creditor countries benefit from the reversal of trade surpluses; exports from developing countries will decline, and imports, especially of capital goods, will rise. Thus recycling provides the financial underpinnings for solving at least a part of the U.S. trade imbalance.

As a counterpart for acceptance of this scheme by creditors (or to make it more acceptable, in case of unilateral action), debtors would have to sustain the budget improvement and to liberalize the scope for foreign direct investment. Debtors might be tempted to dissipate the resources into a restoration of consumption after so many years of deprivation. But that would be unacceptable. Tough-minded fiscal measures and broad-based liberalization of investment opportunities are the quid pro quo for the suspension of resource transfers.

It is worthwhile asking how banks would deal with a recycling situation. The immediate reaction of banks to a recycling proposal is entirely negative, but the concerns are largely exaggerated and lie mostly in the accounting area. Of course, compared with a bailout by the World Bank, recycling is thoroughly unattractive, but compared with default by all Latin America, recycling is strictly preferred.

Individual banks would take one of three steps. They might manage their receivables directly in local currency, clearly the route for banks now in the debt-equity swap business for their own account or for banks that sought to expand their activities in debtor countries. Rather than funding themselves by deposit taking, they will use their own capital in the form of interest payments in local currency. A second group of banks might use their local currency receivables by having them managed by major host country financial institutions—banks, money market funds, or funds that invest in real assets.

A third group of banks would try and sell off their claims to avoid high transaction costs. This would typically be the case of small banks. They would sell their claims to investment funds. These funds (like the Korea Fund or the Brazil Fund, which was just offered on the New York Stock Exchange) sell shares to the public at large and use the proceeds to buy assets in the debtor country. Buying claims from banks, possibly at a discount, would be a natural way of increasing the return to their shareholders.

It is instructive to go through the details of how banks would use the recycling funds to appreciate that what happens is basically a transformation of short-term, illiquid debt into long-term investment. That is an essential step in strengthening the possibilities of long-term growth in debtor countries, avoiding the recurrent bouts of rescheduling with the attendant, massive flight of capital.

A scheme such as this could be likened to reconstruction programs similar to those administered after World War I or World War II. It would extend over a decade or so, and ultimately, creditors would be able to recover their principal and accumulated earnings with a guarantee of no frivolous losses of exchange.

Return of capital would almost certainly be one of the favorable consequences of a recycling proposal. On the resource side financial stability would be enhanced, thus removing one reason for capital flight. In addition, the sharp reduction in foreign exchange requirements for debt service would open the door to the large flow of imports required to sustain growth.

Today asset holders must wonder whether growth and debt service will be reconciled. As a result, they hang on to their dollar positions even in the presence of extraordinarily high real interest rates. Paradoxically, if debt service could be recycled, debtors may well have enough inflow of private capital so that it can actually pay creditors a major part of debt service in dollars. Conversely, if creditors are then adamant, private capital will stay abroad, and creditors, in the end, risk getting nothing. Just as deposit insurance stabilizes banks, so recycling stabilizes the macroeconomy in a situation with two equilibriums—one with capital moving out and the economy deteriorating; the other with capital flowing in and the economy returning to growth and financial stability.

Conclusion

People today generally recognize that a resumption of growth and anything near full debt service are incompatible. Even moderate proposals acknowledge that at most only a portion of debt service can be transferred without prejudicing the opportunities for growth. That raises the question of how the rest of debt service is to be handled: one answer is that international financial institutions must assume an increasing role.

This is, indeed, the banks' position as they ask for guarantees on any new money to be committed. Of course, increasing the commitments by international agencies raises questions about equity: why bail out banks in Latin America rather than provide poverty relief in Africa?[8] Discussion around these issues is going in circles. In the meantime a debtor country like Mexico, having taken the first step toward growth in the form of fiscal stabilization, must move on or else face the risk of sliding back.

Bibliography

Buiter, W. and T. N. Srinivasan. "Rewarding the Profligate and Punishing the Prudent and Poor: Some Recent Proposals for Debt Relief." *World Development* 15, no. 3 (1987): 411–17.

Bulow, Jeremy and Kenneth Rogoff. "The Buyback Boondoggle." Brookings Papers on Economic Activity, 1988.

Cardoso, Elianna and Rudiger Dornbusch. "Private Capital for Economic Development." In *Handbook of Development Economics*, edited by Hollis Chenery and T. N. Srinivasan. New York: Elsevier Science Publishing Co., 1987.

Corden, Max. "An International Debt Facility." IMF Staff Papers, September 1988.

Dooley, Michael. "Buy-Backs and the Market Valuation of External Debt." IMF Working Paper. Washington, D.C.: International Monetary Fund, 1987.

Dornbusch, Rudiger. Background paper to *The Road to Economic Recovery*. New York: Twentieth Century Fund, 1989.

———. "Policy and Performance Linkages between LDC Debtors and Industrial Countries." Brookings Papers on Economic Activity, 1985.

——— and F. Modigliani. "Easing the Mexican Interest Burden." *Wall Street Journal*, January 3, 1989.

Feldstein, Martin. "International Debt Service and Economic Growth: Some Simple Analytics." NBER Working Paper no. 2076, 1986.

Froot, Kenneth. "Debt Buy-Backs." Massachusetts Institute of Technology, 1988. Mimeograph.

Krugman, Paul. "Market Based Approaches to Debt Reduction." NBER Working Paper no. 1987, 1988.

Lessard, Don and John Williamson, eds. *Capital Flight and Third World Debt*. Washington, D.C.: Institute for International Economics, 1987.

Rodriguez, Carlos. "The Strategy of Debt Buy-Backs: A Theoretical Analysis of the Competitive Case." International Monetary Fund, 1988. Mimeograph.

Williamson, John. *Voluntary Approaches to Debt Reduction*. Washington, D.C.: Institute for International Economics, 1988.

4

Market-based Approaches to Debt Reduction

Paul R. Krugman

Much of the privately held debt of developing nations trades at large discounts on the secondary market; table 4–1 indicates the recent extent of these discounts for the major debtors. It is natural that participants in financial markets have sought to find ways to turn these discounts to advantage, and not surprising that some countries have sought to use the secondary market as a way to reduce debt. There is still widespread confusion, however, about the economics of debt buybacks. At one extreme, some enthusiasts have claimed that schemes such as debt-equity swaps offer a way to reduce debt and to attract capital inflows simultaneously, all at no cost to the country; on the other side, some critics have charged that all debt buybacks are nearly pure transfers from the countries to the creditors that will aggravate rather than alleviate the debt problem.

TABLE 4–1

SECONDARY PRICES ON DEBT OF DEVELOPING COUNTRIES, APRIL 1989
(percent)

Debtor Country	Percent
Argentina	16.00
Bolivia	10.00
Brazil	34.75
Chile	58.75
Colombia	55.00
Mexico	42.50
Peru	5.00
Venezuela	35.50

SOURCE: *LDC Debt Report*, April 10, 1989.

This issue has become urgent with the recent and sudden turnabout in U.S. policy toward third world debt. While details of the Brady plan are still fuzzy, it is clear that large-scale debt buybacks, facilitated by guarantees from international agencies, are at the plan's core. Yet no simple guide exists to the preconditions necessary for such a plan to succeed, and much of the public discussion seems vague if not actually erroneous.

This chapter, therefore, presents a sort of primer on the economics of debt buybacks. It offers a survey of the major kinds of buybacks and an analytical framework for assessing their impact on debtors and creditors. While the principal focus is on the logic of buybacks rather than on the details of actual schemes, the chapter also briefly discusses some experience with buybacks to date and offers a preliminary assessment of the Brady plan.

Much of the discussion in this chapter takes the form of presentation of simple numerical examples designed to illustrate key points. While actual or potential policy makers are sometimes offended by a seemingly playful approach to serious issues, thought experiments— for that is what the examples are—are the only way to cut through the fog of confusion that surrounds many of the issues in international debt. Nor are the benefits of clear thinking purely abstract. As I will describe below, the attempted Mexican voluntary debt reduction of early 1988, which was in a way a trial run for the voluntary debt reductions that are apparently the core of the Brady plan, was disappointing for reasons that could have been (and were) precisely predicted by economists using the kind of simple examples that form the backbone of this chapter.

Types of Buybacks

All the schemes for "voluntary," market-based debt reduction involve an attempt to exploit the large discounts on the secondary market as a way to reduce debt cheaply. This, however, does not mean that all buybacks are the same. Much of the confusion regarding debt-reduction schemes arises from the fact that there is more than one kind of buyback. What matters for the economic analysis is not so much the mechanics of the buyback as the ultimate source of the resources for which the debt is exchanged; it is this that largely determines who gains and who, if anyone, loses.

From this perspective, there are four major types of voluntary debt-reduction scheme. We begin by asking whether the repurchase of debt is financed with cash or involves an exchange of one long-term asset for another. If the buyback is for cash, we ask whether the cash is supplied from outside—as in the Bolivian debt relief of 1987—or is supplied by the country itself. Thus we have two kinds of cash buyback: externally financed or domestically financed. If the buyback takes the form instead of an asset swap, we ask whether the asset that is traded for existing debt is another debt instrument, such as an exit bond, or some quite different asset, as in a debt-equity swap. (See the appendix for a discussion of debt-equity swap.) Thus we have two kinds of asset exchange as well.

The key question we want to answer is that of the welfare effects of each kind of scheme. While these depend crucially on the type of buyback, they also depend on two other aspects of the situation. First is what I will call "appropriability": the share of any increase in the debtor's *ability* to pay that will be reflected in its actual repayments. Second is the "incentive effect": the extent to which a reduced debt burden enhances the country's likely ability or willingness to repay the remaining debt. The role of each of these factors will become clear during the discussion below. For now, I will simply assert the basic welfare analysis in the form of a table, shown as table 4–2. This table lists the four basic types of debt-reduction scheme, classified by the kind of asset for which existing debt is exchanged; it contains four columns of information.

TABLE 4–2

Welfare Effects of Alternative Buyback Schemes of Developing-Country Debt

| | | | Effect on Welfare of: | |
Asset Exchanged	Preconditions	Factors	Creditors	Debtors
Cash, supplied externally	None	None	Increase	Increase
Cash, generated domestically	None	Low appropriability	Increase	Decrease
		High appropriability, low incentive	Decrease	Increase
		High appropriability, high incentive	Increase	Increase
New debt	Seniority	Low incentive	Decrease	Increase
		High incentive	Increase	Increase
Other assets	Additionality	Low incentive	Decrease	Increase
		High incentive	Increase	Increase

The first column, labeled preconditions, shows necessary conditions for the scheme to reduce debt in the first place. Thus a debt-for-debt swap will reduce debt only if the new debt can be credibly established as senior to the old debt; a debt-equity swap will reduce debt only if the investments that are financed by the swap are additional to those that would have taken place without it.

The second column indicates the factors that determine who benefits from a given type of debt-reduction scheme. In the simplest case, that of an externally financed buyback, both creditors and debtors always gain (although the distribution of the gains between creditors and debtors depends on the specifics). In the most complex case, that of a buyback using domestically generated cash, the result depends both on the appropriability of resources and on the importance of incentives. In the case of either a debt-for-debt swap or a debt-for-equity swap, the size of the incentive effect is the only crucial variable.

The third and fourth columns, finally, indicate the effects of debt-reduction schemes on the welfare of creditors and debtors. The obvious point is that not all buybacks are alike. Some schemes benefit creditors at debtors' expense, while others do the reverse; only in certain circumstances can both be made better off.

The structure of this chapter may now be seen as one of justifying and explaining table 4–2. To do this, we begin with an analysis of the simplest case, that of a buyback using externally supplied cash.

Externally Financed Buybacks. Much discussion of the debt problem is marked by two evasions that get in the way of understanding. First, official rhetoric, and to some extent that of the banks, has been unwilling to recognize explicitly the strong possibility that the countries will not in fact pay all that they owe. While the reasons for avoiding saying this outright are understandable, it is impossible to discuss the debt problem usefully without acknowledging the real possibility of non-payment.

Second, much official and bank discussion is based on the premise that the secondary market prices of debt represent a highly unrepresentative and uninformative market. There are in fact reasons to suppose that, owing to the distorting effects of bank regulation, the secondary market gives a biased estimate of the expected loss on third world debt—although it is as possible to argue that secondary prices are too high as that they are too low. Again, however, the starting point for any rational discussion must be the acknowledgment that the large discounts on debt reflect a realistic appreciation of the possibility of non-payment.

As a first pass, then, let us suppose that the secondary price of debt actually reflects the expected payments of the debtor country. Notice, however, that these are only the *expected* payments: it is obvious in practice, and crucial in understanding the economics of buybacks, that the actual extent to which countries can or will repay their debt remains highly uncertain.

It will be helpful to refer to an explicit numerical example in the course of this chapter. As pointed out earlier, the use of this kind of hypothetical example to discuss serious real-world issues may offend some. Yet it can be an invaluable aid in clarifying the issues.

Imagine, then, a country that owes $100 billion. We suppose that the present value of the country's future payments is uncertain. With a probability of one-third, optimism will be vindicated, and the country will be able to make payments whose present value covers the value of its debt; call this the "good state." With a probability of two-thirds, however, the country pays a present value of only $25 billion; call this the "bad state." The expected payment from the country is thus $(^1/_3)$ x 100 + $(^2/_3)$ x 25 = 50. Absent any buyback scheme, the country's debt will sell at 50 percent of par.

Let us also provisionally imagine that the probability of the two states is independent of the country's debt burden. This amounts to assuming away temporarily the incentive effects that will play a key role in the analysis of some debt-reduction schemes. For the analysis of an externally financed buyback, however, this is not crucial.

Consider, then, the effects of a debt buyback financed by cash donated from some third party. To bring out the points most clearly, we first imagine that this third party—call it the World Bank—commits itself to reducing the debt to a level that the country will be able to pay with certainty, that is, $25 billion, which means that it must buy off $75 billion of debt. The effects of a more realistic, smaller buyback will be considered below.

The effects of the buyback are shown in table 4–3. We ask, in sequence, the following questions: What is the effect of the buyback on the secondary market price of debt? What is the cost of the buyback to the World Bank? What is the effect on the welfare of the country? What is the effect on the private creditors?

1. *The effect on the secondary price:* An externally financed buyback leaves the country with a smaller debt but with an unchanged ability to pay; thus the secondary market price of the remaining debt will rise. In the extreme example considered here, the buyback is so large that the remaining debt is certain to be fully repaid; thus the secondary price rises to 100 percent of par.

2. *The cost of the buyback:* Marginal sellers of debt must be indifferent between holding on to the debt and selling it. Since everyone knows that the secondary price will rise to 100 percent, the repurchase must

TABLE 4–3

EFFECTS OF A HYPOTHETICAL BUYBACK OF EXTERNALLY FINANCED
DEVELOPING-COUNTRY DEBT

	Good State	Bad State
Before buyback		
Probability	1/3	2/3
Receipts of creditors	100	25
expected receipts = 50		
secondary price = 0.5		
After buyback of 75		
Receipts of remaining creditors	25	25
Receipts by sellers of debt	75	75
expected total receipts = 100		
secondary price = 1.0		
cost of buyback = 75		
gain to initial creditors = 50		
reduction in expected payments by debtor = 25		

take place at par—the buyback costs $75 billion.

3. *The benefit to the country:* In the absence of a buyback, the country would expect to pay $50 billion. With our large buyback, these payments are reduced to $25 billion in both states; thus the country's expected payments are reduced by $25 billion. (This ignores the possibility that there may be an additional gain to the country resulting from the elimination of the necessity of default. I will return to this issue below.)

4. *The benefit to the creditors:* Absent our large buyback, the creditors would expect to receive only $50 billion. With a large buyback, they will instead receive the full value of the debt—some because they sell out to the World Bank, others because the reduced debt can now be repaid in full. Thus the expected payment rises from $50 billion to $100 billion—a $50 billion gain.

Simple as this example is, it illustrates two important points about attempts to provide debt relief by buying back and canceling third world debt. First, such relief is typically very expensive, because the more debt relief is expected, the higher the price that the creditors will demand for their claims. Second, much of the benefit of the buyback goes to the creditors rather than the debtors—a point that has been forcefully argued by Bulow and Rogoff,[1] among others. In this particular example, two-thirds of the World Bank's outlay effectively goes to the creditors rather than to the debtor.

The result that much, perhaps most, of any externally financed buyback goes to benefit creditors rather than debtors seems to be a strong argument against this use of the resources of the international community. Is there any counterargument that can be made? The main one seems to be the following: suppose that debtor countries face additional costs that are not captured by their external payments if they must default. These might include disruption of their trade, closure of future access to international capital markets, and so on. Then to the extent that debt buybacks reduce the probability of outright default (which they will almost always do, if we recognize that realistically there are more than two possible states of nature), the benefits to the debtor may be larger than are suggested here.

Nonetheless, it remains apparent from our discussion that buybacks that use externally supplied cash look uncomfortably like relief for the private creditors rather than the debtor, making this a dubious use of public resources. In practice, schemes for debt relief—including what can thus far be discerned of the Brady plan—generally attempt to supply the externally provided funds as part of a package intended to shift the benefits more fully to the debtor. The key to these packages is that the external funds are used to provide guarantees to the issue of new debt in exchange for old. We will consider such mixed schemes later. First, however, we turn to the pure case of a repurchase of debt financed entirely by the issue of new debt.

Debt Swaps. In a debt swap, a country issues new debt and either exchanges this new debt directly for the existing debt or sells it and uses the proceeds to repurchase debt on the secondary market. In either case, the effect is to substitute new debt for old.

While debt swap schemes, usually taking the form of offering creditors "exit bonds," have attracted considerable attention, there remains a widespread failure to appreciate the key precondition for such swaps to work: the new debt must somehow be made *senior* to existing debt, giving it a prior claim on the country's payments. To see why this is necessary, consider what would happen if the new debt were expected to be treated in the same way as existing debt, so that in effect it would be thrown into the same risk pool. Then the new debt would immediately sell at the same discount as the old debt, preventing any net reduction in debt. Suppose, for example, that debt sells at a discount of 50 percent. An issue of $10 billion (in present value) in new debt would sell for $5 billion; this money could be used to repurchase $10 billion of old debt, but the overall debt burden would not be reduced.

For new debt to sell at closer to par than old debt, purchasers must somehow be assured that they will receive priority in the disbursement of available funds. In the attempted Mexican debt swap of early 1988, the selling point was that the new debt would take the form of bonds, which in Mexico have thus far been exempt from the rescheduling and new money calls that have been placed on bank debt. In other exit bond schemes there is a promise that the new bonds will be exempt from new money calls. In some proposals for debt relief, such as that of John Williamson,[2] partial World Bank guarantees are expected to confer seniority on the guaranteed debt, on the grounds that countries will be less willing to default on international agencies than on private creditors.

In practice, the attempt to confer seniority on new debt is problematic, and difficulties in doing so may constitute a central obstacle to attempts to provide market-based debt relief. For now, however, let us suppose that it is possible to assure purchasers of new debt that they will receive first call on repayment, and examine the implications of a debt buyback financed by issue of new, senior debt.

Consider again the numerical example introduced earlier in this chapter. A debtor country can pay its full debt of $100 billion with probability of one-third, but will pay only $25 billion with probability of two-thirds. As in the first example, the country sets out to repurchase $75 billion of its original debt; however, it now does so by issuing new debt that receives first claim on available resources.

The results are shown in table 4–4. In order to buy back the $75 billion in old debt, the country needs to issue $25 billion in new debt; its net debt falls to $50 billion. To show why this is the size of the required

---

TABLE 4–4

EFFECTS OF A HYPOTHETICAL PURE DEBT SWAP OF NEW DEVELOPING-COUNTRY DEBT FOR OLD, WITH NEW DEBT SENIOR TO OLD DEBT

	Good State	Bad State
Before debt swap		
Receipts of creditors	100	25
expected receipts = 50		
secondary price = 0.5		
After debt swap of 25 new debt for 75 old debt		
Receipts of holders of new debt	25	25
Receipts of holders of old debt	25	0
expected receipts of new creditors = 25		
expected receipts of old creditors = 8.33		
secondary price of new debt = 1.0		
secondary price of old debt = 0.33		
change in expected payments by debtor = –16.67		

swap, we need to show what happens to the secondary price. Since the new debt will be paid first, it will be fully repaid in either state, so that there will be no discount on the new debt. In the bad state, however, the new debt will receive all of the repayment, leaving nothing for the old debt; since holders of the old debt will be repaid only with a one-third probability, the secondary price of old debt falls from one-half to one-third. It follows that $25 billion of new debt can be swapped for $75 billion of old.

The welfare effects of this transaction are quite different from those of an externally financed buyback. The expected payment by the country falls from $50 billion to $33 $1/3$ billion. This gain comes at the expense of the original creditors, who see the expected value of their claims fall by the same amount.

A buyback financed by the issue of new senior debt appears, then, to benefit the debtor at the expense of its creditors. As before, some readers may worry that this result depends on the large size of the assumed buyback, which eliminates any repayment on old debt in the bad state. It is straightforward to show, however, that the same basic result occurs when the buyback is smaller.

The upshot of this analysis seems to be that a debt swap in effect expropriates the original creditors. Thus one might think that creditors should always be opposed to allowing the establishment of the seniority of new debt that makes such swaps possible. The conclusion that the creditors lose, however, depends on a key assumption that now needs to be relaxed: that the country's ability or willingness to repay is independent of the size of the outstanding debt.

In reality, for several reasons a large nominal debt burden may impair a country's ultimate ability to repay debt. First, a debt that is so large that the country is unlikely to be able to repay in full acts like a high marginal tax rate on efforts to expand the country's foreign exchange earnings: the bulk of any improvement will go to benefit creditors rather than the country. Second, because the debt burden may ultimately appear as a tax on domestic capital, it thus acts as a disincentive for domestic investment. Third, to the extent that an inability to pay debt leads to a confrontational or disorderly default, the result may be to reduce eventual payment to less than the country might have paid had a reduced debt been agreed on in advance.

For all these reasons, a reduction in creditors' nominal claims on a country will normally be offset at least in part by an increase in the probability that the country will pay the remaining claims. (In the numerical example we have been using, a lower debt level will be offset in part by a higher probability of the good state occurring.) At very high levels of debt, the incentive effect may be so strong that a reduction in debt will actually increase the debtor's expected payment.

A diagram (figure 4–1) will help us visualize this. On the horizontal axis we show the present value of a country's debt obligations; on the vertical axis, the expected present value of its future debt service. If the country had a low initial level of debt, it would be expected to repay that debt in full; thus the expected value would lie along the forty-five–degree line. At higher levels of debt, however, there would be an increasing probability of default, and thus expected payments would lie along a curve like CD, falling increasingly below the forty-five-degree line. At sufficiently high levels of debt a higher level of indebtedness would actually be associated with lower levels of expected repayment. This curve, which presents an obvious analogy to the Laffer curve in tax analysis, can be described as the debt Laffer curve.

The point is now the following: if a country is so hopelessly in debt that a reduction in that debt will actually increase its expected payments—that is, if it is on the wrong side of the debt Laffer curve—it is in the interest of creditors to allow the creation of new senior debt that permits a reduction in overall indebtedness. The reason is that in this case the improvement in the country's prospects outweighs the cost to existing creditors of having their claims subordinated to the new debt.

FIGURE 4–1
THE DEBT LAFFER CURVE

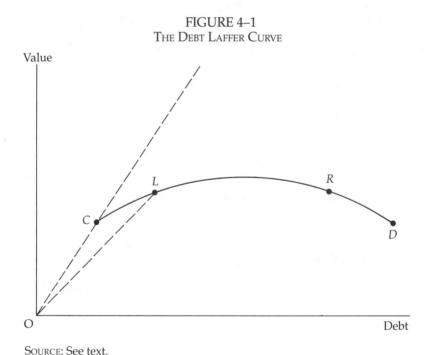

SOURCE: See text.

TABLE 4–5

HYPOTHETICAL DEBT SWAP OF NEW DEVELOPING-COUNTRY DEBT FOR OLD,
WITH INCENTIVE EFFECTS

	Good State	Bad State
Before debt swap		
Probability	1/3	2/3
Receipts of creditors	100	25
	expected receipts = 50	
	secondary price = 0.5	
After swap of 25 new for 50 old debt		
Probability	1/2	1/2
Receipts of new creditors	25	25
Receipts of old creditors	50	0
	expected receipts of new creditors = 25	
	expected receipts of old creditors = 25	
	secondary price of new debt = 1.0	
	secondary price of old debt = 0.5	

Table 4–5 illustrates a borderline case in which issuing new, senior debt reduces a country's net indebtedness without any cost to its existing creditors. In the table it is assumed that a reduction in our hypothetical country's debt from $100 billion to $75 billion is enough to raise the probability of a good state from one-third to one-half. Thus such a debt reduction would leave expected payments unchanged at $(^1/_2) \times 25 + (^1/_2) \times 75 = 50$. What the table shows is that such a debt reduction could be achieved by issuing $25 billion in new, senior debt. The remaining old debt would receive nothing in the bad state but be fully paid in the good state, so its secondary price would remain 0.5, implying that the new debt could be used to buy off $50 billion of the old debt, reducing the net debt to $75 billion. This transaction would leave the country better off at no cost to the existing creditors. Obviously if the incentive effects of a debt reduction were even larger, a debt swap would make everyone better off.

Two important points need to be made about the debt Laffer curve analysis. First is that the analysis has nothing to do with the question of whether a debt-reduction scheme is advantageous to the *debtor*. A pure debt swap is always beneficial to the debtor, if it can be arranged. The question is instead whether it is possible to devise a scheme that benefits both the debtor and the creditor, other than through contributions from a third party.

Second, the mere existence of a secondary discount does not guarantee that debt can be reduced without harming the creditors. At point

L in figure 4–1, there is a secondary market discount (with the price of the debt measured by the slope of OL), but debt reduction will hurt the creditors. Only if the debt is so large that it puts the country on the wrong side of the curve, as at point R, is there potential for mutual gain.

This means that the question of where countries really are on the curve is a controversial one. I will return to this question below but for now simply point out that the analysis given here points to the two key issues in debt swaps: how to establish the seniority of new debt and how to convince the existing creditors that allowing the issue of new debt is in their interest.

Domestically Financed Buybacks. Externally financed buybacks are possible only when a third party is prepared to contribute resources; debt swaps work only if seniority can be established. Thus far only Bolivia has managed to assemble external donors to repurchase its debt, and nobody has managed to establish credibly the seniority of new debt over old. There remains, however, the option of self-financed debt reduction, in which a country simply buys back its own debt on the secondary market.

Even this debt-reduction method is not automatically available. The sharing provisions under loan agreements, by requiring that payment be made on all bank debt equally, prevent direct purchase on the secondary market. Creditors have been willing to acquiesce in a variety of indirect buybacks, however, notably those that (as we will see) often result from debt-equity swaps and from the use of reserves to collateralize new debt.

As we cut through these disguises, we should consider the effects of a direct use of cash generated by a country itself to repurchase some of its debt at a discount. This cash may come from existing foreign exchange reserves or it may be generated through trade surpluses. In a certain sense, even cash supplied by third parties to finance a buyback can be considered domestically generated, since the cash *could* have been given directly to the country; thus the use of that cash to buy back debt represents a choice not to spend it on something else.

At this point a new issue arises. This is the issue of "appropriability": how much of a dollar that is used to buy back debt would have gone to the creditors if not spent in this way—that is, how much of a marginal change in a country's resources can be appropriated by the creditors? At one extreme, some believe that debt-service payments by debtors are generally independent of their resources, that there is near-zero appropriability. In this view, a dollar spent on reducing debt will reduce payments to creditors only in those favorable states of nature when the country would have been able to service its debt in full in any case. This view has been starkly stated by Bulow and Rogoff.[3] At the other extreme, others believe that creditors essentially take as much from a country as it can manage to pay and that this includes foreign exchange reserves. In this view, with near-complete appropriability, a dollar spent on debt reduction is a dollar that creditors cannot seize in adverse states of nature, and the debt repurchase therefore reduces payments in bad as well as good outcomes.

The effects of a self-financed debt repurchase depend crucially on the degree of appropriability. With near-zero appropriability, the re-purchase acts just like an externally financed repurchase, which, as we have seen, typically conveys most of the benefit to the creditors rather than to the debtor. In this case, however, the cost of the buyback falls on the debtor itself. The result is therefore to reduce the debtor's welfare.

Suppose that we were to run once again the thought experiment shown in table 4–3, with a buyback reducing the debt from $100 billion to $25 billion. As we saw, the cost of this buyback is $75 billion, even though the expected payments from the debtor fall by only $25 billion. Now suppose, however, that the debt repurchase is financed by the country itself. Then the country will have expended $75 billion to reduce its expected payments by $25 billion, experiencing a net ex-pected loss of $50 billion. Clearly, if appropriability is really very close to zero, self-financed debt repurchases are a very questionable policy.

In contrast, suppose that the resources used to repurchase debt are in effect taken away from what might have been paid to creditors in unfavorable states of nature. Suppose, for example, that by using up its foreign exchange reserves through repurchases a country puts itself in a position where its creditors have to forgive debt in the event of an unfavorable movement in export prices, whereas the country would have been forced to cover the shortfall out of its reserves otherwise. In a case of near-complete appropriability, a self-financed debt repurchase is similar in its effects to debt repurchase financed with issue of senior debt. (In corporate finance, where creditors can seize the assets of bankrupt firms, near-complete appropriability is the rule. This is why repurchase of debt at a discount is normally prohibited.)

Table 4–6 shows the effects of a debt repurchase in a case where the resources used to make the repurchase would otherwise have been available to service debt. Specifically, the table supposes that the $25 billion that would otherwise have been available to service debt in the "bad state" is used to repurchase debt instead. The effect is to reduce debt to $25 billion and expected payments from $50 billion to $8 $1/3$ billion. Thus there is a net gain to the country of $16 $2/3$ billion, exactly as in the case where the country issued $25 billion of senior debt.

The case shown in table 4–6 appears to show a clear net loss to the creditors. As in the case of debt reduction financed by senior debt, however, a sufficiently strong incentive effect can reverse the result.

TABLE 4–6

EFFECTS OF A DOMESTICALLY FINANCED HYPOTHETICAL BUYBACK OF
DEVELOPING-COUNTRY DEBT, ASSUMING COMPLETE APPROPRIABILITY

	Good State	Bad State
Before debt repurchases		
Receipts of creditors	100	25
expected receipts = 50		
secondary price = 0.5		
After repurchase of 75 old debt		
Receipts of creditors who sell out	25	25
Receipts of remaining creditors	25	0
expected receipts of creditors who sell out = 25		
expected receipts of remaining creditors = 8.33		
secondary price of debt = 0.33		
change in expected payments by debtor = –16.67		

The case of debt buyback financed from domestic resources has
created a great deal of dispute—understandably so, since it is simultaneously the easiest kind of debt-reduction scheme to implement in
practice and the most ambiguous in its results, being potentially either
beneficial to the creditors at the expense of the debtors, to the debtor at
the expense of the creditors, or beneficial to both. The case of domestically financed buybacks, however, should not be overemphasized. By
its nature it cannot be a major contributor to the solution of the debt
problem. Almost by definition, problem debtors are short of cash. Thus
they cannot be expected to finance large-scale debt relief out of their
own resources. Nor are large donations from third parties, which could
have been given as direct aid, likely to be forthcoming. If there is to be a
large-scale attempt at voluntary debt reduction, it will generally have to
take the form of an asset exchange rather than an outright cash purchase.

The Mexican Debt Swap

In December 1987 Mexico announced a plan to retire a part of its old
debt in return for new debt. The new debt consisted of twenty-year
zero-coupon bonds, with the principal but not the interest guaranteed
by U.S. Treasury obligations purchased by Mexico with its own foreign
exchange reserves. Mexico was prepared to issue up to $10 billion of the
new debt and hoped, given the roughly 50 percent discount on its debt
in the secondary market, that as much as $20 billion of old debt could be

canceled.

It is immediately apparent that this plan essentially packaged together two transactions described earlier in this chapter: in effect, Mexico engaged in a debt swap while at the same time using domestically generated resources to buy its debt back.

Clearly one would expect the new bonds to have a higher secondary price than other Mexican debt because of the collateral provided. At the interest rates then prevailing, the collateral turned out to be about 20 percent of the value of the debt; thus with other Mexican debt selling at about 50 percent of par, the new debt should have sold at a minimum of 70 = 50 + 20 percent.

What Mexico hoped was that the new debt would actually sell at a substantially higher price than this, perhaps close to 100 percent. To command such a premium, the new debt would have had to promise credibly some degree of seniority over the old debt. Mexican officials attempted to suggest that this would, in fact, be the case: they claimed in particular that the new bonds would be excluded from any future restructuring agreements and that the loans exchanged for these bonds would be excluded from the base for any future requests for concerted lending.

The upshot of the attempted debt swap is well known by now. When bids offering to exchange old debt for the new bonds were received, only $3.67 billion exceeded Mexico's minimum acceptable price; these loans were exchanged for $2.56 billion of the bonds, backed by $492 million in collateral. When account is taken of the fact that the interest rate on the new bonds exceeded by a small margin that on rescheduled bank debt, the transaction turns out to have reduced the present value of Mexican obligations by almost exactly the same amount as would have been achieved by a straight cash buyback using the same amount of resources.[4] In essence, because the Mexicans failed to establish seniority, their debt swap degenerated into a domestically financed buyback.

The major lesson of the Mexican experiment seems to be how difficult it is to establish seniority. This is not a good omen, because no voluntary debt-reduction scheme can get very far unless it involves the issue of new assets that the market regards as senior to the existing debt.

The Brady Plan

At the time of writing no specifics were available on the proposed implementation of the announced intention of Treasury Secretary Nicholas Brady to seek voluntary debt reduction aided by funds from Japan, the World Bank, and other sources. Some news reports suggested that an overall debt reduction of perhaps 20 percent would be sought, but it was unclear whether this represented a serious target.

It is nonetheless instructive to consider some illustrative scenarios for what the Brady plan *might* look like.

A reasonable guess is that the Brady plan would essentially consist of the following: the World Bank and others would offer participating creditors a guarantee in return for reductions in interest rates. A full guarantee would offer a safe asset to creditors who accept; thus they should be willing to accept a reduction in the interest rate proportional to the secondary market discount. The working of a partial guarantee would be more complex; if guaranteed debt can be made credibly senior to unguaranteed debt, however, creditors might still be willing to exchange an interest reduction close to the secondary discount in return for the guarantee.

In round numbers, at the time that the Brady plan was announced, the total commercial bank debt of troubled debtors was about $300 billion. The average secondary market price of that debt was only about 30 percent.

I will calculate the effect of several hypothetical "Brady plans" along the same lines as the numerical calculations used to illustrate the argument throughout this chapter. To do this, I must specify the distribution of payments that give rise to the observed secondary market prices. This will be arbitrarily specified as follows: there is a .125 chance that the countries will pay their debt in full and a .875 chance that they will pay a present value of only 20 percent of the face value, that is, $60 billion. These probabilities are taken as fixed, so that no allowance is made for the debt Laffer curve. Obviously, predicting the outcome of a guarantee scheme depends on getting the shape of the distribution of repayments right, so that the results reported here are to be taken as illustrative rather than definitive.

We consider, then, a plan in which an external party guarantees a portion of the debt, demanding as a quid pro quo that the interest payments on the guaranteed debt be reduced in proportion to the secondary market discount. First we ask what happens if this guaranteed debt does not have any perceived seniority over unguaranteed debt. Table 4–7 shows the effects of two alternative scenarios: a modest plan in which enough debt is guaranteed to reduce interest payments by 20 percent and an ambitious plan in which the attempt is made to reduce debt service by 50 percent.

Even in the modest plan it turns out to be necessary to guarantee more than 30 percent of the debt, approximately $91 billion. The reduction in debt service on the guaranteed debt leaves more available for the remaining debt, so that the secondary price rises from 30 to 34.3; correspondingly, creditors gain more than $13 billion. The debtor countries,

TABLE 4–7

"BRADY PLAN" FOR DEVELOPING-COUNTRY DEBT
WITHOUT SENIORITY FOR GUARANTEED DEBT

	Reduction in Interest Payments	
	20 percent	50 percent
Percentage of debt guaranteed	30.4	95.0
Value of debt guaranteed	91.2	285.0
Secondary price of unguaranteed debt	34.3	47.3
Gain to creditors	13.1	51.9
Reduction in expected payments by debtors	7.5	18.8
Expected losses of guarantor	20.6	70.7

SOURCE: Author's calculations.

meanwhile, have a reduction in *expected* payments of only $7.5 billion. These gains are paid for by the risk assumed by the guarantor: the guarantor's expected losses are $20.6 billion.

An ambitious plan to reduce debt service by 50 percent is much more expensive. It is necessary to guarantee 95 percent of the debt—$285 billion. The reason is that the reduction in the debt burden drives the secondary price up from 30 percent to more than 47 percent. Correspondingly, the more ambitious plan produces large gains for the creditors, almost $52 billion.

These are not encouraging numbers. A 20 percent reduction in interest payments is too small to do debtors very much good, while the size of the guarantee and the implied risk for a 50 percent reduction are far greater than seems politically palatable at this point. The case looks even worse if one bears in mind that the guarantee authority could be used in other ways that might yield a substantially greater payoff to the country.

Matters look quite different if the guaranteed debt can somehow be given senior status. Table 4–8 shows what happens if the debt that is guaranteed is strictly senior to the unguaranteed debt. First, we note that the secondary price of unguaranteed debt falls instead of rising, because of its subordination (a result that might be reversed with the debt Laffer curve). Second, as a result, the interest-rate reduction that can be demanded in return for a guarantee is greater, so that less debt need be guaranteed—slightly less when only a 20 percent reduction in interest payments is sought, much less when a 50 percent reduction is the objective. Third, given our assumptions, the guarantor actually assumes no risk, since even in the bad state the debtors are able to pay

TABLE 4–8

"BRADY PLAN" FOR DEVELOPING-COUNTRY DEBT
WITH GUARANTEED DEBT SENIORITY

	Reduction in Interest Payments	
	20 percent	50 percent
Percentage of debt guaranteed	27.5	65.5
Value of debt guaranteed	82.5	196.5
Secondary price of unguaranteed debt	27.5	23.8
Gain to creditors	–7.5	–18.8
Reduction in expected payments by debtors	7.5	18.8
Expected losses of guarantor	0	0

SOURCE: Author's calculations.

enough to cover the guaranteed loans. In other words, the guarantee is in a sense unnecessary: the seniority that is assumed to be conferred by the guarantee actually does all the work.

This immediately suggests that *if* seniority can be established for guaranteed debt, the guarantees can be partial rather than complete; they would essentially serve the function of validating the debt rather than providing protection. If this could be done, a quite limited amount of guarantee authority could "convoy" enough new debt to achieve significant reductions in interest payments.

The problem is, however, that seniority is difficult to establish, especially as banks have not so far been willing even to consider the principle of subordinating their debt to guaranteed debt.

The definite possibility therefore exists that an attempt to rely on partial guarantees will produce a result similar to the Mexican experience: the attempted large debt exchange would degenerate into a much smaller cash buyback, which would principally benefit the creditors rather than the debtors.

On the whole, it is difficult to be very sanguine about the prospects for effective debt relief through voluntary mechanisms on the scale that would make the Brady plan a success.

Appendix: Debt-Equity Swaps

The main text of this chapter does not discuss debt-equity swaps, even though these have in fact been the form taken by the most extensive debt repurchases to date. There are two reasons for this. One is that the potential for debt-equity swaps is not large enough for them to play a key role in any large-scale program of voluntary debt reduction. The other is that a debt-equity swap is a fairly complex transaction that is difficult to analyze and has been the subject of a fair amount of financial mysticism. Rather than muddy the waters early in the analysis, I have therefore separated the awkward discussion of these confusing transactions from the main line of argument.

Debt-equity swaps have been the subject of some extravagant claims: some have asserted that they simultaneously attract capital inflows while reducing a country's external liabilities, a neat trick if it could be arranged. In reaction against these claims, some analysts have argued that in practice debt-equity swaps are seriously harmful. To assess this debate, we must once again do some more explicit analysis than is usual in this area.

The first point to make is that under no circumstances does a debt-equity swap constitute a net capital inflow. The country simply exchanges one kind of external liability for another. The exchange may be desirable, as I will discuss in a moment; but it does not add to the supply of domestic savings or, what is equivalent, contribute resources toward debt service and thus diminish the trade surplus that the country needs to run to service a given debt.

The second point is that reducing debt is not the same as reducing external obligations. When equity is substituted for debt, foreigners relinquish their claim on a future stream of debt service in return for a claim on a future stream of repatriated earnings. The present value of the stream of repatriated earnings may or may not be smaller than that of the debt service.

Before getting to the question of the effects of a reduction in debt offset by an increase in foreign equity holdings, however, I will address a prior issue. It is unfortunately not always the case that allowing equity purchases to be paid for with debt actually leads to a net increase in foreign equity holdings. This is the issue of "additionality": how much of the equity investment that takes place through debt-equity swaps is actually an increase over the investment that would otherwise have taken place?

The most obvious case in which debt-equity swaps fail to produce additional equity investment occurs when the foreign investor resells the equity to a domestic investor and takes his cash out of the country again. Such "round-tripping" is not unknown, but it is well understood, and actual debt-equity schemes at least attempt to police such abuse.

The more important problem case is one in which a debt-equity swap is used to finance an investment that would have taken place anyway. Perhaps the most notorious example is that of the Nissan plant in Mexico, which by all accounts would have been built even if no swap program had been available. Given the opportunity to finance the project via a swap, however, the firm naturally took advantage of the lower price, paying for its investment with debt acquired at a discount rather than cash.

What happens when a debt-equity swap fails to generate additional equity investment? The answer is that the swap degenerates into a repurchase of debt using domestically generated resources. Nissan's use of a debt swap meant that the money that it would otherwise have supplied to the central bank did not arrive, requiring the central bank to spend more of its foreign exchange reserves to pay for imports than it otherwise would have.

We should also note that at best, if additionality is 100 percent, a debt-equity swap represents zero net capital inflow. To the extent that the swap has less than 100 percent additionality, then, the result is de facto a capital *outflow*.

Thus a high degree of additionality is necessary if debt-equity swaps are to constitute a real exchange of assets. Otherwise they degenerate into a disguised cash buyback of debt, typically at less favorable terms for the debtor than could have been realized through an explicit buyback.

Suppose, however, that a debt swap program can be devised to ensure a high degree of additionality. The next question is whether the program actually reduces a country's external liabilities in the sense that it reduces the present value of payments to foreigners. The answer is not necessarily: it depends on the size of the premium that foreigners are willing to pay to convert their debt to equity. This in turn, while it depends on a number of factors, must depend crucially on the same consideration that determines the feasibility of debt reduction through issue of new debt. That is, investors must form a judgment on the seniority of equity as opposed to debt.

This sounds like a strange issue, since in ordinary corporate finance debt is always senior to equity. If this were the case for countries, then a debt-equity swap would typically *increase* the present value of a country's liabilities to foreigners. The current argument, however, is that debt is a source of controversy and bitterness that equity is not and that Latin American nations might default on their debt while still honoring the property rights of direct investors. This is possible, although it is only a decade since multinational firms rather than banks were the chief targets of radical rhetoric in the third world.

If equity can be made credibly senior to debt, then debt-equity swaps will have the same qualitative effects as debt-for-debt swaps in which the new debt is senior. This is why the welfare effects are shown as equivalent in table 4–2.

Even if a debt-equity swap fails to reduce a country's obligations, it may still have some other advantages. The repatriation of profits will ordinarily come later than the debt service it replaces, so a successful swap will improve a country's liquidity position. Debt-equity swaps can also serve other purposes, such as encouraging foreign direct investment that is expected to yield side economic benefits. Against this must be put the risk that the net effect of such swaps will be a net capital outflow, as well as the typically adverse budgetary implications.[5] My own guess is that in practice a sufficiently high fraction of debt-equity swaps will degenerate into cash buybacks on unfavorable terms that they will do the debtors more harm than good. Even if one disagrees with this assessment, the potential for debt-equity swaps is clearly limited. The main thrust of schemes for large-scale use of the market to reduce third world debt is on a combination of externally financed buyback and debt-for-debt swaps. In particular, as discussed above, the Brady plan apparently will consist largely of an attempt to reduce debt through swaps with new debt, partially backed by guarantees from international agencies, rather than through swaps for equity.

Bibliography

Dooley, Michael. "Buy-backs and the Market Valuation of External Debt," IMF Working Paper. Washington, D.C.: International Monetary Fund, 1987.

Froot, Kenneth. "Buybacks, Exit Bonds, and the Optimality of Debt and Liquidity Relief." *International Economic Review* 30: 49–70.

Krugman, Paul. "Financing vs. Forgiving a Debt Overhang." *Journal of Development Economics* 29: pp. 253–68.

5

Institutional Approaches to Debt Relief

Eugene H. Rotberg

My observations concern the implementation of the recent initiatives announced by U.S. Treasury Secretary Brady.

The sooner a transaction is executed, the better. Expectations are quite high. In truth, it does not really matter whether the transaction results in reduced cash outflows from the debtor countries. Indeed, most debt-relief and debt-reduction proposals will not significantly affect how much debtors will actually pay, over and above the funds lent to them. In fact, in recent years many debtors have met only about half their debt-service obligations with the balance coming from the banks themselves. The great advantage, however, of Secretary Brady's initiative is that it is politically attractive in debtor countries. If executed, the initiative could forestall calls for moratoriums or cessation of payments; it could diffuse radicalized movements in countries with fragile political systems. It could even contribute to the repatriation of flight capital because it could remove the uncertainty of protracted, contentious negotiations for new money packages. The initiative certainly will be described in a manner implying that the burdens on the debtors are lessened. That, too, is an assumption that may be just as important as the real effect on the borrowers' actual external payments.

More dangerous would be not to execute any meaningful transaction or to create exaggerated expectations that, by magic, debtors will be supplied with cost-free funds to buy back enough debt so that what remains will result in a meaningfully lower burden than what they are now paying. That will not happen given the magnitude and the sources of the funding.

I cannot overemphasize that point. Most commentators on Secretary Brady's initiative confuse two separate aspects: the actual cash-flow burden on the debtors and the accounting effect of the transaction on the creditors. They are *not* reciprocals of each other. In part, the confusion occurs because the terms *debt relief, debt forgiveness,* and *debt reduction* are typically used to describe the effect on the creditors' books and records after the transaction is executed and do not describe the before and after actual cash flows of the debtor net of new lending.

The way that debt reduction is recorded on creditors' books has little to do with the actual cash savings of the debtor, that is, the net interest paid by debtors to creditor banks. For example, if a debtor owes $4 billion in interest in a given year on $40 billion of debt outstanding and the banks, as part of a "new money" package or otherwise, increase their exposure during the year by lending $2 billion, which is then "round-tripped" back to them, then the net burden on the debtor's economy in that year is $2 billion, not the $4 billion interest "paid." Therefore, if subsequently a debt-reduction or debt-relief scheme were implemented (even assuming it costs the debtor nothing) enabling the debtor to buy back half its debt or reduce its interest payment obligations by half, the debtor, still required to pay interest on the remaining half, would have the same *net cash outflow burden* as before the transaction was executed. It is only under conditions when the debt-reduction or debt-relief transaction is cost free, large enough, or accompanied by new lending that debt-reduction schemes will, in fact, result in a lesser burden than before. This is not to say that the initiative is insignificant, for there are great political and image advantages to debtors. Moreover, it is in the interest of creditors to reflect the real world accurately. Let us not pretend, though, that when we finally reflect reality accurately, we are changing it.

One of the reasons why the proposals now being considered are not likely to have a substantial cash-flow impact is that international institutions have constrained resources and competing demands for money or guarantees from other developing countries that are not part of the debt crisis and that have performed well. They cannot overcommit limited resources to a few countries in Latin America. International financial institutions also have to satisfy constituencies in the credit markets that look carefully at their policies and programs in deciding whether to provide finance.

I therefore have urged, in other writings, the establishment of an affiliate that would take guarantees and similar credit enhancement to the heavily indebted debtors off the books of the development banks, so as to avoid a direct link between their callable capital and their debt-crisis interventions. Otherwise, given the financial structure of the World Bank and other development institutions, their role is not likely to be significant in financial terms. Indeed, I suspect that whatever the World Bank makes available by way of permitting buybacks of debt, the debtor country will receive that much less from the bank, almost dollar for dollar, for imports of goods and services needed to maintain their exports.

Whatever the transaction under the new initiative, it will not remove the need for debtors to make painful adjustments in their own economies; indeed, it will likely increase those pressures as credit enhancement or guarantees from international financial institutions will assuredly be accompanied by the imposition of considerable conditions. Indeed, whatever the financial engineering, it should be staggered over time in a manner in which the economic reforms can be monitored over the medium and long term. In short, the international institutions must retain the continuing leverage to insist on structural economic reform in debtor countries.

Despite what I think will be a rather modest role compared with the magnitude of the problem in the very heavily indebted countries, the risk remains that in some countries official guarantees or credit enhancement could be quite significant. Then a debtor country might have little alternative but to default to official institutions during periods of stress if those institutions have assumed a substantial portion of the debtors' remaining external indebtedness. In short, therefore, substantial commercial risk should always be left with the banks so that during periods of stress—high interest rates, recession, deterioration of terms of trade, falling (or rising) prices for oil—a cushion remains; that is, potential commercial bank lending can still be called upon.

It is obviously not possible here to describe what specific measures the World Bank or any affiliate might take to maintain its high credit standing because that would depend very much on the magnitude of what is guaranteed, how it is guaranteed, and whether the World Bank's risk is increased or stays the same. That is, is there additional risk, or is the form of risk merely changed? There are ways, however, both to lay to rest any question about the bank's credit standing in the markets and, at the same time, to increase the penalty to commercial banks so that Secretary Brady's initiative would not be considered a bailout by the development institutions. If, for example, there were guarantees that were exercised and "put" to the World Bank upon receipt of payment from the World Bank, those funds might be re-lent immediately to the World Bank at three-month U.S. Treasury bill rates for, say, twenty years. For want of a better term, since the World Bank has been put in play, as the saying goes, we might call that a "poison put." It seems fair enough, and, in any event, an opportunity loss (from the diminished return should the put be excercised) is a concept that, as we all know, is not recognized as a standard acceptable accounting priniciple and, therefore, would not show up as a loss on commercial banks' books.

I have one final point—perhaps the most important that I would raise here. There is a lot of talk about issuing bearer bonds in connection with debt-reduction or debt-relief schemes. If these were issued in large amounts, I would send up a red flag, because those bonds would be traded outside the banking system. If defaulted on, as they well might be if the amounts were significant, pension funds, insurance companies, and private individuals are not likely to be nearly so malleable as commercial banks in working out the problem. Instead, they will go to court and will attach the assets of the debtor or insist on being bought out by the banks. I am surprised the Federal Reserve has not commented on this aspect. For my own part, I simply am not comfortable with a lot of developing-country bearer bonds floating around outside the banking system in a litigious society like the United States.

PART TWO
Evaluations of Approaches
to the Debt Problem

6

Capital Flight and Reflight

Allan H. Meltzer

The most important thing to emphasize about the debt problem, monument to the policies of the debtor countries, is that, unless these policies are changed, long-term growth in those countries will not resume, the debt problem will continue, and major sources of funds will not be available. For the foreseeable future, the principal source of funds likely to be available to the debtor countries is the money that left them as flight capital. Despite whatever efforts may be made, there will not, in my opinion, be anything close to an equivalent amount of funds provided by world taxpayers through various international agencies or governments or by the commercial banks.

Although the Brady plan has been introduced because of the well-recognized failures of the Baker plan, those failures are not often spelled out. In my mind, they were that the plan did not provide incentives, either for the debtors or for the creditors, to move forward. The debtors received little new money to implement reforms. Most of the money they received went to pay interest. The creditors received $15–20 billion a year from the debtor countries in the form of interest payments, so they had little incentive to change the system.

The failure of the Baker plan was, I believe, predictable. We now have the beginnings of a Brady plan, which has been compared to an offer to sell fire insurance at bargain rates in a town where half the people are arsonists. That refers to one aspect of the Brady plan—the idea that we can guarantee some of the debts and improve the circumstances of the debtors by doing things like guaranteeing debt and forgiving debt. That neglects the fact we want to emphasize, that the principal source of new funds and of growth for these debtor countries has to come from reform of their policies and the repatriation of capital to them. Guarantees will not do that.

The problem, as I see it, is that the Brady guarantees are a first step in the shift of liability from debtors to taxpayers of developed countries. How long that path is and where it leads, the Brady plan does not spell out. But no one could possibly believe that the Brady plan is a one-time solution that will be the end of the story. At best, its terminal point is uncertain.

In this and other respects, the debt problem is reminiscent of the savings and loan problem experienced in the United States. It started with bad accounting and failure to mark to market. A few guarantees were added in the hope that small steps would lead to big results. Conferences were held, with many proposals of the kind we have heard. This, too, is reminiscent of the S&L problem. Almost anything is done except discuss the principal problem—namely, What steps will the debtor countries take to reform their economies so that they can grow and service their debts?

Some comparisons between countries are instructive. In 1980 Korea had 50 percent of its GDP in debt, while Brazil had 30 percent. About eight years later, Korea had a debt ratio of 30 percent, and Brazil 40 percent.

During that period, consumption grew in Brazil and Korea at the same rate, so Brazil was not squeezed, although it had some ups and downs. Its consumption is now about the same annual average rate higher than Korea's, but what a difference. In Brazil, which has had spurts of export growth followed by declines, exports have grown at an average rate of $6\frac{1}{2}$ percent, in comparison with 16 percent in Korea. That difference explains why Korea is in a strong financial position and Brazil is not.

Brazil could put itself in a strong financial position. When Brazil wants more export growth, it has been able to get more export growth. If Brazil had the will or the interest, it could solve its problems. That could be said of many other countries as well. The Brady plan does not give the countries the incentive to grow.

In addition, the Brady plan twists the creditors' arms to get them to surrender two clauses designed to protect not just creditors but also the institutions of the world capital market. These protections are the sharing clause and the negative pledge clause. If these clauses can be put aside easily at the behest of governments, there will not be much of a capital market in the future. The clauses prevent involuntary subordination and side arrangements that favor one creditor over another. The principles of debt contracts have been developed over a long time and should not be pushed aside just to take some steps that are ill defined and ill advised.

I do not, however, favor the status quo. The Council of Economic Advisers report for 1989, which I helped to prepare, proposed two steps that are part of the Brady plan. I favor both of those steps.

First, the Brady plan should make new lending conditional on governments' structural reforms, not on the vague and often unkept promises that have characterized much of the past system of so-called conditionality. Second, it should leave the outstanding debt to the banks. It should say to the banks: The problem is yours—do with it what you can; negotiate the remaining value.

These proposals can solve two of the major problems that existed under the Baker plan. First, much of the lending done under the Baker plan was used ultimately to pay net interest to the creditors. Second, there was little incentive or financial aid for reform in the debtor countries and little incentive for the creditor countries to make any progress toward eliminating the debt. Both of those problems, I believe, would be removed.

Each year under the Baker plan, the banks collected about $15–20 billion of new money. Meanwhile, the debtors received loans from the IMF, the World Bank, the governments, and the Paris Club, but little of it was available for new investment or restructuring.

To repeat my earlier comment, whatever solution to the problem may be proposed, the main source of capital for the debtor countries is capital that their citizens hold abroad. There will be no lasting solution until the problem of capital flight is resolved. Reforms are required in the debtor countries to remove many of the price and wage controls, to set exchange rates at market levels, to begin to privatize some industry, to reduce subsidies, and to pay for retirement homes for old generals or for places for them to hide. Taxes on exports will have to be removed, or at least progress will have to be made toward modifying them.

If these and other reforms are taken credibly, then there will be hope of capital reflight, and much of the problem will go away. If they are not taken, then the likely result will be more capital flight, and the problem will remain or worsen.

7

The Key Question Is
the Bargaining

Stanley Fischer

Allan Meltzer talked about Brazil, but countries such as Mexico, Colombia, and Chile made genuine adjustment efforts and cannot regain access to commercial financing. Mexico and other countries face a debt overhang that seems seriously to inhibit a return to growth. These countries have a real need for some means of tackling the debt overhang.

The situation was not viable before. The Brady plan is replacing something that was not working and was breaking down. The strategy had to be changed. One question that could be asked is, however, Is the Brady plan a breakthrough or an evolution of the Baker strategy?

The elements of the Baker strategy were: first, growth-oriented adjustment by the developing countries; second, money from the international financial institutions; and, third, new money from the commercial banks. By 1987, the Baker strategy had evolved to include voluntary market-based debt reduction as a component in the financing packages.

Viewed against that background, the Brady plan and related initiatives—such as the Japanese and Mitterrand initiatives—are, in fact, evolutionary. In regard to the first element, the initiatives' most important common requirement is serious adjustment programs by the developing countries. The point made by Allan Meltzer and others must be emphasized: Debt-service relief and debt reduction should be considered only for countries that make a serious effort to straighten out their domestic economies.

What worries me about this approach is that the enthusiasm for it seems so great there is a tendency to make premature decisions about countries with very different records. Debt reduction is seriously discussed for some countries where reforms began only yesterday and are still in prospect. Mexico and others, however, have been implementing reforms for some time. For countries in these very different situations, very different methods of conditionality and very different timings of debt relief are needed. But the emphasis in the Baker plan on adjustment by the debtor countries is the key element in the Brady initiative as well. This is one reason for the intervention of the international financial institutions in the process.

The second common element is that the international financial institutions will give roughly the same amount of money as they would have given if the Baker plan had continued. So that element is the same.

The third is that there is to be a contribution from the commercial banks. The emphasis of the Baker plan on new money, however, is being changed. Overall, the Brady plan is really an evolution of rather than a revolution in the Baker strategy. Nonetheless, it is an extremely important change.

The next issue is the adequacy of the financing available under the Brady plan, which is very tricky. Starting with the official money that is mentioned for debt reduction, the U.S. Treasury has given a number around $25 billion. This amount seems to be made up first of IMF loans, possibly of about $7 billion over the next three years. Then, $4–5 billion of World Bank adjustment lending that would have taken place in any case will be available for debt reduction. That makes $12 billion from the two sources. Finally, additional support for interest reduction of $6 billion over three years from each institution is included. As far as I know, neither institution has actually made a decision on that additional funding, but it appears to be in the Brady proposal and the subsequent testimony on it.

The Japanese have stated they will provide 4^1\!/_2$ – 5 billion dollars in support of debt reduction. Again, the question is whether that is over and above their normal foreign aid budgets. That money may be provided to the indebted countries in some other form.

The extra money for debt reduction is therefore relatively small. Treasury calculations that such relief would reduce the debt by about 20 percent for a group of thirty-nine countries are probably a little high. In addition, a 20 percent number is a bit misleading because the great bulk of debt reduction would go to fifteen or seventeen heavily indebted countries that are responsible for the major share of commercial bank debt.

It is quite possible that still more money will be needed to make this process work. If current market prices of debt reflect the lower limits of the cost of buying it back, then there must be something else in the minds of those pushing the Brady plan.

The next issue is what the additional contributions to reducing debt might be. Obviously, they would have to come from the commercial banks in some way. The big question is the official role of creditor countries' governments, although the answer may seem already to have been given—namely, the IMF and the World Bank will put up money. Actually, the IMF, the World Bank, and those governments will play another important role in coordinating the debt reduction process.

Previous debt packages used the concept of critical mass—namely, that the IMF and the World Bank would not disburse money until sufficient money had been pledged from the commercial banks and other sources to assure the official agencies that the financial gaps would be covered. Under the previous system, we did not disburse until the critical mass was there.

That system put power in the hands of the international financial intermediaries, because their money would not be given unless the other parties contributed. It also, of course, put power in the hands of the banks, because nothing would flow until they had agreed to whatever package was on the table.

The U.S. Treasury has argued that this process should be changed so that the IMF and the World Bank could disburse money without assurances by commercial banks or others to cover the financing needs envisaged in an analysis of the country's economic prospects. Implicitly, this system states that the official community will tolerate arrears from the debtor countries as part of the bargaining process with the commercial banks.

It is difficult to foresee how that process is going to work out. The arrears do accumulate. Allowing arrears might be fine for a while, but it would not reduce the countries' indebtedness in any way. It would put pressure on both the banks and the countries. This system would not make clear, however, how the bargaining will come out or whether it will facilitate the type of deal that Allan Meltzer mentioned, in which the banks and the debtor countries would sort out their problems, with the help of official financing as a catalyst.

That uncertainty will pose very tough questions for politicians and policy makers. Since banks in the industrialized creditor countries would not be happy with the accumulation of arrears, political pressures could be expected to build. And the debtor countries would not be happy with an unresolved financial situation that dragged on for years. Therefore, the precise process by which new financing is worked out will have to be handled sensitively and carefully by the creditor governments and the international financial agencies.

That procedural question has not been resolved. Treasuries around the world have conceivably figured out how to handle new financing and not explained how for bargaining reasons. If I were in their position, I would not explain it either. But maybe it is a tough issue whose handling has not yet been worked out.

In any case, this process has started. The IMF has announced that it

THE KEY IS BARGAINING

will disburse significant amounts of money in support of debt reduction to Mexico, which is about to negotiate with the banks. Political pressures will be brought in from the developing countries, from the debtor countries, from the banks, and from others in the next few months as this bargaining takes place. How these pressures are resolved will be very interesting and very important.

That is the key question in the Brady plan—the bargaining strategy. Official money will be used to oil this bargaining process in a variety of ways. The question is, What will be the official attitude toward the bargaining between debtors and creditors?

Turning last to capital flight, Allan Meltzer has the good fortune of never having lived in a country with capital controls. I have. When you have taken your money out of a country like that, the last thing you want is to bring it back. Allan is quite right that these countries should take measures to prevent further capital flight. The notion that this stock of money will come back without a long record of good economic management is not plausible.

I think of capital flight as a multiplier on successful adjustment programs. If they work, then more financial resources will be gained over time than had been expected. If they do not work, more will be lost than was predicted.

The policy implications of my view and of Allan's are not very different—namely, debtors need to straighten out their economies. The only question is whether responsible governments can count on significant amounts of capital flight coming back as they plan where to get financing in the next few years. My guess is that expecting capital return within two or three years would not be wise. It is something to aim for and to hope for but not to rely on.

8

The Need for Debt Concessions and Forgiveness

Jim Kolbe

As we consider proposals to address LDC debt, the case of Mexico serves as a good starting point for discussion. The recent development of airline competition in Mexico illustrates the rather extraordinary changes taking place in that country, which few in this country have focused on. The airline that we were familiar with as Aeronaves de Mexico, now known as Aero Mexico, is providing real service in that country. Mexico is now wide open to competition in the air service industry. American airlines are scrambling to get a place in this new market, and the Mexican airlines are actually competing on an international scale with better service. They are actually finding luggage and delivering it where it is supposed to go!

The acceleration of privatization and the opening of the marketplace in Mexico are, I think, very, very important. They started in the last administration under President de la Madrid and have accelerated enormously in the current administration of Carlos Salinas de Gortari. For the first time, Mexicans have had continuity in economic policy from one administration to the next.

I liken what is occurring in Mexico to what happened in Korea a decade or a decade-and-a-half ago, although Mexico is in some ways much further along. Tariffs and many other regulatory barriers are much lower there than in Korea. In other areas, such as selling of state-owned industries, Mexico is not as far along.

By and large, Mexico has made extraordinary progress in the past few years and appears poised for further gains. I think in the near future we will see important things happening in Mexico. An explosion of growth will take place in that economy. But, of course, debt remains as Mexico's curse and albatross, and any optimistic outlook for the future will depend on how this "monster" is tamed.

The Baker plan has been given a bad rap in the press, and it is true that it now seems "passe." But it deserves a more decent burial. The Baker plan may not have accomplished what it set out to do, but it did do what it needed to do. It gave everyone some breathing room. It allowed the banks to do what they needed to do to stabilize the situation and build their loan–loss reserves, which in most cases now equal approximately what is needed to cover the debt in some developing countries.

Now it is time to go on to the next step. But the Baker plan does not take us there. Whatever plan replaces Baker, it must have some significant debt forgiveness and concessions.

Not long ago, Senator Bentsen, chairman of the Senate Finance Committee, said, "I don't think some of these countries are ever going to pay off their debt unless there is some reduction in interest rates and in principal. There has to be some forgiveness and concessions."

That is a broad statement, but a fairly broad consensus is developing in Congress behind it. Whatever we do, we have to find some way of reducing the principal and interest payments for these countries, because that is the only way that growth can resume. Mexico is in a position now where growth absolutely must take place. And they've built the foundation for it to occur. It's up to us to help provide the building blocks.

Of course, I am interested in Mexico because it shares a border with my home state of Arizona. But I also believe Mexico will be the foundation stone of our debt plan. Mexico has been the model debtor country under the Baker plan. Mexico has done everything asked by the IMF, the World Bank, the commercial banks, and the U.S. government. It has undertaken reforms and in some areas has gone much faster and much further than anybody expected—in the reductions of import licensing requirements, for example, and the elimination of structural trade barriers.

Quantitative restrictions that used to apply to 100 percent of imports, now apply to less than 12 percent of imports, and only in the automotive, pharmaceutical, and computer sectors. In addition, tariff barriers have been reduced across the board. The highest tariff went from 100 percent to 20 percent, and the average tariff is now between 10 and 12 percent, the lowest in the developing world.

Beyond this, Mexico has sold off hundreds of its state-owned industries. It has closed many others.

With tough wage and price controls, Mexico has reduced inflation, from 160 percent a year in 1987 to an annual rate slightly less than 19 percent in 1989. At the same time, Mexico has reduced its public spending by an amount that equals about three Gramm-Rudmans. We still have several years to go before we get to our first Gramm-Rudman, and Mexico has done three in much less time.

Clearly, growth is now critical to Mexico. But growth is also in the interest of the United States. Mexico has to create jobs for an explosive population that adds 1 million new workers to the market each year. If it cannot, or if Mexico becomes politically unstable, those people will come across the border—legislation notwithstanding.

In the long run, these programs will reverse capital flight. On a temporary basis, by the way, it has been reduced—since January 1, 1989, Mexico has had a slight net capital inflow. For the time being, these flows have been constant and stable and signal that Mexican investors are awaiting an answer to the debt question. Maintaining this stability will require sticking with these programs of reform and showing real progress on debt negotiation.

Otherwise, the economic problems that Mexico faces will become political problems, and their political problems will become the United States' political problems.

9

The View of
the Banking Community

John B. Haseltine

Speaking for the banking community at any time is an unnatural act because the banks of the world are so incredibly diverse. It is hard to get two or three bankers in a room to agree. Nevertheless the Institute of International Finance has over the past two or three years made an effort to achieve consensus among the banks that are continuing in the process of assisting developing countries. The banking community has had several reactions to the Brady proposals.

First, the banks generally welcomed the speech and the earlier comments by President Bush in December. That was the first time in a very long while that this issue was mentioned at the highest levels of the U.S. government. There was recognition, finally, that this is not the type of crisis it was six years ago. It is an ongoing foreign policy problem, an ongoing international economic policy question, and an ongoing concern to major banks around the world, although the banks are not hostage to it as they were six years ago.

The problems now seem to be too complex, too broad, and too politically charged to be left just to the debtor countries and their private creditors. And so the focus on the question by the U.S. government and other governments has to be welcomed.

The banks welcome the Brady proposals because they reflect the best of the strategies we have had since 1982. They recognize that the obligation for solution to the debt problem rests first and foremost with the debtor countries themselves. Let me say that the problem in these countries is to get their policies and their structures up to date, to modernize their economies, and to put themselves in a position to compete with others in the developing world.

It is clear that the rest of the developing world enjoys market access today, and many countries are racing ahead. Countries that fail to adjust more speedily than they have so far will be left hopelessly behind.

Second, the Brady proposals keep the banks and the countries in the spotlight and oblige them to negotiate. Negotiation can be a long and arduous process, but it has been successful. When countries have made financing requests, the banks have responded in almost every case.

Third, the proposals recognize that each country at each time is unique, that each situation has to be addressed as it is, and that flexibility is required by all parties concerned.

Fourth, it continues the requirement that an IMF program be in place and that the IMF and the World Bank have the ability to monitor the situation on behalf of the creditor banks.

The banks welcome some of the new features in the Brady plan. The first is the recognition that voluntary debt reduction is a viable idea. It is a recognition that such reduction is going on. Over the past three or four years, debt of some $30 billion has been reduced through debt-for-equity swaps and other programs. It is a recognition that there is already a shift, if you like, in exposure from the private sector to the public sector, particularly in the fifteen Baker plan countries. The total exposure of the banks was something like two-thirds or a bit more in 1982, and it is coming down to 55 percent and still declining. So the shift is occurring, and the debate should be over the best use of public resources, given what is happening.

The banks also welcome the increase in the number of countries eligible under the Brady proposals. Many of us would like to see the smaller countries that have taken difficult steps enjoy the new resources that will become available. In the management of the debt problem, we have waited too long to come to agreement with the larger countries and then applied that from case to case to smaller ones. For many of these smaller countries, a small amount of World Bank and IMF resources will have a catalytic effect and produce a significant lessening of commercial bank debt. The total numbers may not be large, but they provide substantial relief for the individual countries. So this phase of debt strategy should focus more on the medium- and smaller-sized countries.

The banks also welcome the secretary's comments on debt-for-equity programs and on the need to come to grips with the capital flight problem. The banks have no magic solution to that problem. Clearly, it is the governments' policies that count, but the creditor countries must continue to apply pressure on the debtor countries to take specific actions that will help reverse the flow of capital.

A stop-go, stop-go debt-for-equity program is worse than no debt-for-equity program. But if a country is willing to build a debt-for-equity program into its medium-term fiscal/monetary planning, even starting on a small scale, the patrimony issues and the monetary and fiscal issues can be dealt with, but not from one day to the next. The banks therefore want such a program to be built into structural plans. Debt-for-equity is one of the best signals to banks and private investors abroad that a country is determined to welcome investment and to become creditworthy again.

Perhaps the greatest concern of banks is that the secretary's March 10 speech and subsequent comments said little about support for new money. Many of the smaller countries will probably not have access to new bank money, on a voluntary or involuntary basis, for a long time. Because the larger countries will continue to need new money, however, questions arise: How can both the provision of new money and debt reduction be done? Can both be done? Can there be substantial debt reduction? We hear from some quarters that debt reduction will not be substantial for the larger countries because the resources are not there. But can we have some debt reduction and at the same time get the banks to lend new money?

That is an open question. In the financing of Brazil last year, we saw that a country that manages well can, in fact, accomplish both. But if the countries rush to the trough for debt relief, and three or six months later come back to the banks for some new money, that simply will not work.

It will also be very difficult for countries such as Colombia, which was referred to earlier, that just wish to come for new money in the form of balance-of-payments financing. Whether the banks should or should not have made balance-of-payments loans as a result of the OPEC surpluses is arguable. They have learned their lesson, however, and will not make available large-scale balance-of-payments financing for a very long time. Banks need a menu of options, both on the new money side and on the debt-reduction side.

The banks are also concerned about the lessening of the linkage between IMF disbursements and actions by banks. We have heard the expression "tolerance of arrearages," which puts fright into a banker's heart and is the kiss of death for general waivers. General waivers and tolerance of arrearages are like oil and water.

We can probably assume the banks will continue to support a country that has been performing by repaying its obligations and that has a well-founded financing program, which includes a menu of options both for new money and for debt reduction. The banks will not give general waivers. In three or four instances the banking community has given specific waivers for debt-reduction programs, and I believe that will continue to be the case. But there is concern that the official lenders may be going one way, just as the banks are being asked to go another.

There is concern, too, about the stick. We have heard what will happen if the banks do not respond to some preconceived notion of the right amount of debt reduction. In testimony over the past three or four months, I have heard that we are in a honeymoon period and that Congress will wait until the fall of 1989 to act. But if the banks have not responded by then, the regulators will be encouraged to penalize them in all sorts of interesting ways.

That discussion is not very constructive, particularly for countries that will need new money in the future. If debt reduction is not voluntary, there will surely be less response than there has been in recent years to requests for new money in any form.

In the stage we are entering, it is very important to give the right sort of signals to a number of countries. It will be a complex strategy to manage. It will require even more cooperation and coordination than we have witnessed between official creditors and private creditors and between all the creditors on one side and the debtors on the other. For that to happen, everyone will have to give a little, and the very highest levels of our government will have to show a continuing interest in making everyone understand that.

10

Not One Debt Problem
but Hundreds

Slade Gorton

From the point of view of someone who was a critic perhaps, and will be a player at some point in the future, the most overwhelming, the most trenchant single lesson to me in the course of my two years with the Twentieth Century Fund's Latin American debt study was that there is not a single developing-country debt problem—there are hundreds of problems. Between thirty-five and fifty developing countries have some kind of problem with respect to their international debt. In each of those countries, a portion of that debt is likely to be owed to financial institutions in the United States, and very likely a larger portion to financial institutions in other nations or to international institutions. And a significant portion of that debt may well be owed to the government of the United States or to the government of some other nation.

Among these particular challenges, the most serious single challenge is how a specific solution applied to one country, from one group of institutions—whether governmental or private within that country—will affect everything else that happens.

My colleague Jim Kolbe spoke of the primacy of Mexico and of the responsibility of the government there in dealing with an almost intractable problem. I think he is entirely accurate. Mexico has taken many of the steps necessary to put its house in order; whether they amount to three Gramm-Rudmans or not, they are nonetheless overwhelmingly significant steps. But will Mexico feel that a debt relief of, say, 20 or 25 percent, which might be warranted in the abstract, is appropriate if the debt of Peru or Bolivia must be relieved by 60 or 80 percent because it has no ability to pay? Will any lesser figure of debt relief be acceptable in the political system of any Latin American country when another country, by reason of obvious necessity, eventually receives more relief, whether by a joint, bilateral, or multilateral action or by some form of repudiation?

That seems to me to be the most difficult problem of all. It is, of course, appropriate to say that modest actions can have a tremendously positive impact on the economies of small debtors. And, even if those actions amount to eating a substantial portion of a debt by a private bank in the United States, the United Kingdom, or Japan, it will not affect that bank's condition much. It will, however, affect the demands of all of the large debtors of that bank.

It is appropriate to say that each nation ought to be treated differently, and that a nation ought to be treated more favorably if it has undertaken internal economic reforms with some success, if it has tried to keep its payments current, if it has liberal trade policies, and if it is engaged in privatization of government businesses. But the irony is that when it has done all that, then we can say it only needs modest debt relief. The lesson is that debt relief will be greater when the debtor nation is less responsible.

It is not for me to say what the attitude of banks here or elsewhere will be toward future lending. It seems a paradox to believe that there will be any lending in the near future in a nation that receives any private debt relief. The banks in getting themselves into this debt problem ten or fifteen years ago, however, were certainly ignoring the repudiated debts of the 1930s and the 1940s. When the next generation of international bankers comes along, the lessons of the early 1970s will probably be regarded as of no relevance or importance in their decisions.

By breaking out of the increasingly irrelevant set of policies advocated by his predecessor, Secretary Brady offers real hope. More than the report I worked on does, I would encourage in both our private sector and our public sector maximum openness to investment within each of these countries and debt-for-equity swaps.

I agree with Mr. Haseltine that something more than a day-to-day or a week-by-week policy is needed. A very high priority should be given to some form of transfer obligation measured in dollars, which could be turned into an obligation measured in local currency, and used for a constructive purpose when that local currency has been paid.

If we could discount the relationships of negotiations with large countries, we could easily deal with smaller debtors. Until we have a program that appears workable in Mexico and Brazil, and perhaps in Argentina, we will have only worked around the edges of this challenge.

The fundamental question, to which I have no answer, is: How much is required to cause the economies of Mexico, Brazil, and Argentina to begin to grow again? And what will the impact be on private and public entities in the nations required to give that debt relief?

Can we afford to recognize losses—which in many cases have already taken place—in amounts sufficient to make a real difference in those countries? Can we make commitments to make good the balance of those debts and encourage economies in those countries that will help keep those promises? That is the nature of this problem. Even after spending some time on it, I have far more questions about it than answers.

11

Different Treatment of Different Countries?

A Discussion

MR. MELTZER: Two points have not been discussed thoroughly enough. The first is the nature of the resources being discussed. The Brady plan is a bit vague about exactly what is being offered. Stanley Fischer gave the numbers that one hears. Originally, the Brady plan was supposed to provide in the neighborhood of $30 billion worth of new money, of which two-thirds would go to Mexico for three years. That would mean something on the order of $6 billion a year for three years. Depending upon the interest rate, that would pay between 75 and 100 percent of the interest on the Mexican debt.

But the numbers Stan Fischer gave are $12 billion from the IMF and the World Bank and $4–5 billion from Japan—with some question whether that is additional money or total money from Japan. That adds up, at most, to $16–20 billion. So the question is, What will happen? If two-thirds of that $20 billion goes to Mexico, we will not buy a lot with this program. In fact, we are not talking about much of a program. We are talking about reductions in certain standard guarantees and debt contracts and certain guarantees that are going to shift the debt at an even faster rate from private to public hands.

That strikes me as a poor bargain. A proposal ought to tell us at least that there is a chance of getting to the end point and how one would expect to do it. What we are talking about is some help to Mexico for the demonstrable progress it has made, but not enough even to put the Mexican problem on a path toward a solution. I would like to see what the rest of that path is.

People here and elsewhere have talked a lot about the great improvements in the Mexican economy. But a lot of that improvement has been substitution of internal debt. Between 80 and 100 percent of the savings generated in Mexico are needed to pay the interest on the domestic debt. Without further substantial reforms, Mexico will not be in a position to do much, even if it gets the relief that we were talking about, unless it does something about its larger internal problem.

Finally, while the suffering in many of these countries has been severe, most indicators show that Brazil, for example, has a 6 percent per year increase in consumption. Mexico has done much worse than that, but its growth rate is still positive from 1982 to 1986. Considering the numbers in the Brady plan and how far Mexico has yet to go, even though it is one of the leading countries in making progress in this area, we ought to proceed slowly toward guarantees and forced waiving of clauses in old contracts.

If the banks want to waive certain provisions of their loan agreement because of a country's performance, as in the case of Chile, that seems to me their private decision. When the government tries to change those agreements, we put at risk a lot more than we are likely to gain.

Mr. Fischer: About $24–30 billion of official money would be devoted to debt and debt service reduction over the next three years. Of that amount, at least $12 billion and perhaps $17 billion would be additional. But the net increase for buying debt reduction is probably $25–30 billion.

As Mr. Haseltine said, the share of official debt in the indebted countries has been rising and would rise even more under the Brady debt-reduction scheme. For that reason the international financial institutions will be especially concerned about the absolute level of the debt as well as their share of the debt in the future. And that is why the IMF and the World Bank are not likely to provide new funds for debt reduction, unless the other creditors make a substantial contribution to reduce debt.

I would like to amplify Senator Gorton's comment about the problems of different treatment of different countries. Although we naturally focus on the countries that are currently heavily indebted, countries within the World Bank like India and Indonesia that have serviced their debt faithfully and, in the case of Indonesia under extreme difficulty, and whose debt would stand at par if it were traded, are extremely concerned about the debt relief and debt reduction that are being provided.

It will be very difficult to handle that problem within the international community by confining the plans to market-related plans that deal with existing debt traded on secondary markets. That automatically limits the number of countries, but politically it may not contain the problem for very long. That is something that has to be considered.

Finally, I would like to talk about whether it would be unwise for governments to intervene in any way in the contracts between private creditors and debtors. That principle should have been observed in 1982. The notion that governments have not intervened, however, and would be doing something different if they took a stand on the issue of waivers seems farfetched.

This whole process of debt relief has been founded on intervention by the governments since 1982. The problem arose in part because the banks believed that governments would become involved. Everybody knows the famous statement by Walter Wriston that governments don't go bankrupt. That turns out to have been correct. The reason it is correct is that the official agencies have been making sure it did not happen.

I think governments are in this deeply. The notion that we are dealing with nice clean contracts between private creditors on one hand and governments on the other does not fit the current situation. There is bound to be government intervention in these arrangements.

One wants to respect contracts as far as possible, but some stand will be taken, and has been taken, by the Treasury and other official agencies on ways those contracts might be changed.

MR. KOLBE: The question is, How do we get where we want to go? There are obviously differences of opinion, but everybody seems to agree that some action is needed. We have not heard the specific steps to take to get there—who will take the lead, when we will do what, and what the timetable might be. That is very important.

In Mexico, they have substituted internal debt for much of their external debt, and that is a problem. I would point out that their public sector spending as a share of gross domestic product has dropped by more than 10 percent, so they have substantially reduced public sector spending.

I think they have made the kinds of changes they need to make—structural changes in their economy needed for growth. The last required step is some kind of debt relief, some assurance that there will be help for them so that they can move and grow. It is in our interest to give them that.

The toughest problem is how to deal with the debts of the different countries: the debt of Peru, which has been fairly irresponsible; the debt of Mexico, which has made a lot of changes to reform; and the debt of Indonesia, which, as Mr. Fischer pointed out, has been able to service its debt completely.

How do you deal with the problem without rewarding countries that have not taken steps and without penalizing countries that have been completely responsible in servicing their debt from the very beginning?

If all countries are treated the same, some kind of mechanism should reward the ones that have made the necessary changes to reform their economies. They might be given new drawing rights, or perhaps new lending not available to other countries.

MR. HASELTINE: If the official share of the pie does increase because commercial bank debt is greatly reduced through debt-reduction transactions, that would be a good reason for the World Bank to begin considering some innovative ways to attract new bank lending. Although there have been discussions over the years, the timing may now be right to look seriously at some innovative ways for particular countries. These could be nontraditional ways for commercial banks to cooperate with the World Bank, whether by some sort of joint leasing programs, or by insurance pools in which banks, debtor countries, and the World Bank all contribute, or other ways. Techniques are not lacking—the will and the decision on policy have been lacking.

To keep the World Bank "preferred debt," if you like, in the same proportion to total debt it has been the past few years and to keep the commercial banks in the picture, a great deal of thought now has to be given to ways for the World Bank to be a more successful catalyst in attracting new money.

On another point, beginning to tamper with debt contracts would be extremely serious. A much better approach is for the banking community itself to try to bring in line recalcitrant banks that do not want to give waivers on specific operations that the majority of the banking community believes justified. Until we get some experience, I would not like to see the stick being wielded over the banks.

Something else I forgot to mention earlier is that some countries may be reconsidering whether they need their bank steering committees or their bank advisory committees to the same extent. This is a serious problem for the banks. That one group of banks could speak for the entire community has afforded a great deal of protection. If that breaks down and if countries begin to negotiate with the Canadian banks and Canadian government and with the Japanese government and Japanese banks, they are certain not to get waivers, because each part of the banking community will suspect it is somehow being subordinated to another. So if the steering committee process is in question, there will be a greater reluctance to consider waivers.

QUESTION: The debt solution has been discussed as if it involved just the United States, the IMF and World Bank, and the debtor nations, ignoring the G-7 and G-5 nations. Aside from the United States and Japan, how important is the cooperation of a U.K. or a France in the process?

MR. FISCHER: Their cooperation is very important. For one thing, their banks are involved, and I believe that extensive talks are taking place now. I suspect the G-7 will agree on a concerted position soon.

QUESTION: I fully support reforms in developing countries, but what about fiscal policy reforms and interest rates in the United States as they affect third world debt?

MR. MAKIN: If the United States reduced its deficit, there would be a reduction in demands on capital markets. I tend to think the significance of U.S. debt that is 2 to 3 percent of GNP is overemphasized, but if $150 billion is taken out of the pipeline, that would help a little. Congress is obviously deadlocked on the problem of how to do it.

COMMENT: I would agree that the importance of the debt is sometimes overestimated. But the problem is that it absorbs so much of the available capital in the world. We can see that in what is happening as our deficit continues.

We are headed roughly in the right direction, in one way or the other, whether or not we get into long discussions about Gramm-Rudman, about the accounting procedures used on the Social Security reserves, or about a variety of other things. I would agree that the budget summit we achieved is more smoke and mirrors than reality. But we can focus on some positive aspects of it. I think the continuing deficit of the United States is a significant factor in all of this.

COMMENT: If the deficit of the United States would mysteriously disappear tomorrow, the effect on this problem would be minuscule, *de minimis*. The problems do not occur because of foreign lending or because of foreign debt payments. The problems arise in these countries because of the internal policies pursued.

We should try to get our house in order, but it would not make a great difference to Mexico unless Mexico—or Brazil or Argentina—gets its house in order.

MR. FISCHER: I think that's right, but a change in the real interest rate of a couple of percentage points would make a very big difference to the transfers these countries have to make abroad.

12

Debt Reduction, Debt-Service Reduction, and New Money

David C. Mulford

When I spoke on policy coordination and debt in December, I said that we were in the process of reviewing the debt strategy, acknowledging that the problem remained an extremely serious one. Although we had seen significant progress in recent years, there was a good deal of so-called debt fatigue, both among debtor countries and in the commercial banking community. I also made the point that the IMF and World Bank should again make an evaluation of how their resources in supporting debtor nations might be used more effectively. And, finally, I indicated that we thought there should be a stronger emphasis in the future on voluntary market-based solutions for reducing debt and reducing debt service.

Our review process, completed about six weeks later, was an in-depth exercise that confirmed a number of important points. One was that reasonable progress had been made over the past three or four years. Positive growth had been achieved in many debtor countries. There had been some adjustment, significant in certain countries, and a substantial reduction in current account imbalances among debtor nations. Better debt-service ratios were in effect at that time, partly because of the decline in interest rates. Over time, the banks had substantially strengthened their financial positions. Finally, some important policy changes had been made in a number of countries that should have lasting effects—for example, Mexico's decision to join GATT.

At the same time, we clearly were faced with extremely serious long-term problems. Although growth had been established in many of the countries, it was not strong enough to support a sustained recovery among many of them.

Moreover, the reforms that we had seen in many countries were not consistent or comprehensive enough to sustain the kind of recovery that was necessary. Capital flight was still a major problem, with little repatriation of capital except in certain countries where sophisticated markets indicated some return, on a short-term basis in many cases.

Investment is still disappointing. The conditions for both foreign and domestic investment on a substantial scale had not been created. Many countries still maintained too closed an investment regime, and, of course, these problems have a bearing on capital flight repatriation.

The banks, we judged, had been withdrawing at a fairly rapid pace and had been fully serviced during their withdrawal, in part with funds from international financial institutions. Although some important debt reduction transactions were taking place, particularly with debt-equity swaps, the banks' willingness to reduce exposure, in many cases, passed no benefit to the debtor countries.

During the past three years, official exposure, in general through the Paris Club, export finance, and in the international institutions, has risen sharply. There is wide disagreement on the relative exposure levels of commercial banks versus international institutions during that period because of complex problems associated with exchange rate valuation, among other things. But the pattern, I think, was clear: a shift in risk was taking place.

We saw another problem in countries that were taking the difficult decisions to bring in new policies—by undertaking an IMF program and large World Bank loans with tough conditionality. Once these countries had made these difficult policy decisions, they found that under the present methodology the new resources could not be brought to bear quickly enough. Although there are good reasons for this, we regarded it as a serious problem. After economic reform programs had been agreed, long negotiations tended to follow between most of the countries and the commercial banks, during which compliance with the various programs became a problem. Sometimes waivers were necessary to resolve those problems with, for example, the IMF. In general, a disruptive process tended to undermine confidence in many countries, because money was not coming in quickly enough to support the countries during their period of adjustment.

This problem is the result of the way the financing packages were put together. The problem is not entirely produced by the commercial banks but by the general complexity of the situation and by the need to put together resources from the IMF, the World Bank, the Paris Club, and the commercial banks in such a way that all parties feel assured before funds are actually lent. We thought the problem needed reexamination and that it would perhaps justify a revision to strengthen the debt strategy.

Meanwhile, the external debt in general, the debt owed by the major debtors, and, of course, the debt-servicing requirement continued to grow. We were concerned, therefore, about the long-term effects of these patterns on the health and financial stability of the international institutions, because if the trends continued their exposure would continue to rise. At some point, their preferred creditor status might have been questioned. Unless they were willing to go on producing loans larger than the repayments due to them from the various debtors, there might be a risk of arrearage developments with major debtors, with implications for the health of the international institutions.

So we were concerned about what might happen to both the World Bank and the International Monetary Fund and what might be the price for creditor governments. If the tendency to transfer risk continued until the banks withdrew, more or less, the entire debt problem might end on the doorstep of the creditor governments. In short, if the debt strategy continued without alteration, and more resources in due course were added to that approach, one had to ask whether the result would not be more of the same and whether that was really what we wanted.

Our conclusion to all these questions—and I cite them to indicate the comprehensive judgment that had to be made—was that these realities had to be recognized and steps had to be taken to strengthen that strategy, but not at the expense of the basic principles of the strategy. In our view, the general principles of the so-called Baker plan remained both valid and widely accepted by all the various parties. These principles held that there was no solution to this problem without establishing strong growth in these countries, that reform in these countries was essential, that the process begins at home, that there would be a continuing need for external financial support in the period ahead, and that a case-by-case approach appeared to be the most logical.

We also reached the judgment, however, that the approach had to be strengthened and that the key problems I mentioned had to be addressed. In this process, we reviewed a variety of proposals, and we discussed the situation with creditor governments, with debtors, and with international institutions. We sought to find features of proposals, ideas, and viewpoints that could be brought together into a comprehensive effort to strengthen the present strategy.

We also noted that the markets were producing important new developments, largely in debt restructuring. Over the past two years, the debt reduction—that is, a reduction in the stock of debt—that flowed from voluntary transactions between banks and debtors had been taking place on a large scale, though not large enough, of course, to resolve the whole problem. Significantly, that was taking place simultaneously with the provision of new money by the banking system. This seemed to be where we should focus our attention in our attempt to accelerate or broaden that process.

As we arrived at this point, we had certain strategic objectives in mind. One was to deal with concepts and directions and not to put out a blueprint, a made-in-America plan that was expected to be followed in detail by all the participants. That would not have been possible in any case, because the United States does not control all the pieces to this problem. We hold only 19 to 20 percent of the voting power in the international financial institutions. Our commercial banks account for 27 to 30 percent of the outstanding debt of the fifteen major debtors. Obviously, one country, whether it is the United States or Japan or some other, cannot come up with a solution and carry it forward without a major international effort.

Besides, we wanted to create a set of concepts and directions that reflected the views of the many participants we had spoken to. We wanted features that all parties could identify with and support.

At the same time, we wanted to be early enough with these proposals to allow weeks of active and intelligent discussion before the spring meetings of the Interim Committee and the Development Committee and before the meeting of the G-7 ministers, which was set for early April. We felt that the impetus from those meetings must lead us through as short a transition as possible from the old strategy to a strengthened one. If that could not be accomplished, discussions at the spring meeting might be followed by a long recess before anything further happened at the World Bank meetings in the fall. That would be extremely negative.

Finally, we believed it important to conclude the international development banks' negotiations, because the international development banks have a role to play in the debt strategy and represent an important resource for the future.

Among the key elements in our thinking was our decision to try to mobilize more effectively financial support for reforms in the debtor countries. I use the term "financial support" to include both new money and any other transaction that brings in the participation of banks or other institutions. And, of course, it includes both debt reduction and transactions that reduce debt service.

We continued to believe that the IMF and the World Bank had a key role to play in encouraging reform and catalyzing financial support. And we continued to place a strong emphasis on policies and performance among the debtor countries that would have access to the new proposals.

In addition, we wanted to focus more on increasing investment flows—that is, on opening markets in those countries to foreign investment and on giving more attention to capital flight and the need to repatriate capital effectively. Both among the institutions and the debtors, we wanted to encourage thinking about the problem as one that has to be solved, as opposed to simply looking at financing gaps and filling them with new money or rescheduled debt, as has been the case. Although this is a difficult problem, it is very important to pursue, and we plan to give it heavy emphasis.

On the question of financial support, continued new lending by the banks, of course, is very important. Perhaps some differentiation between new lending and old loans will be needed. It is an area for discussion, but we took the view that new money would continue to be important in the future.

At the same time, we wanted to place a strong focus on market-based voluntary debt reduction and debt-service reduction. This involved redirecting existing international institution resources in the IMF and the World Bank to facilitate debt reduction, as opposed to just contributing to more debt and more debt service, as the pattern had been.

In the past, debtors probably doubted that performers were being rewarded. Under this set of concepts, with a set-aside portion of policy-based loans to be used for debt reduction and with additional interest support resources made available for debt-service reduction transactions, performing countries can identify a reward in the form of these additional resources.

Finally, we have to look carefully into the methodology of the institutions. It seems to be widely agreed that we need new thinking on the question of exactly how these pieces will come together.

Another important concept was to encourage the commercial banks to agree to waive legal constraints that impinge upon market-based activity. Some debt reduction has been occurring, of course, but with only partial benefits to the debtor countries. Our view was that a broader range of options was needed with benefits of reduction actually being passed to the debtors. This involved the idea of cash buybacks, for example, discount exchanges, and interest reduction transactions negotiated between debtors and commercial banks—all in this particular case supported one way or another by official resources already in use.

The set-aside concept is a debt-reduction concept. The idea is to set aside a portion of the policy-based disbursements flowing from the IMF and the World Bank specifically for use in transactions that have the effect of reducing the stock of debt. They would include cash buy-backs and collateralized exchanges that take place at a discount.

The interest support concept is somewhat different. There we have in mind a more general pool that has to be defined, and its execution by the IMF and the World Bank have to be worked out. Both institutions are looking at that now. The purpose would be to support interest flows for a short period on a rolling basis on debt-reduction transactions and on restructurings where the emphasis is on reducing the interest rate, and then supporting those flows for a limited period, again at the reduced interest rate level.

Both approaches are necessary, in our opinion, in any effective plan, for two reasons. The first is that we must appeal to the broad community of world banks, some of whom appear willing to undertake transactions in the market that involve a write-down of principal. Other banks, many of them outside the United States, seem to have a strong preference for transactions where, instead of writing down principal, they take a loss on interest, which they see as a less final decision.

If we cannot cater to the two broad options that exist today in the world banking system, then we probably cannot produce a significant result. If we can successfully appeal to both appetites, however, and create the techniques with the leverage we have in mind, then we can make an impact with modest resources.

The second reason is that the debtors themselves need both. If we were to offer only debt reduction, some debt-service reduction would flow implicitly from those transactions over time. But the effect on transfers would not be significant enough to make the impact we feel is necessary in the short term. Hence, both debt reduction and debt-service reduction are needed.

Will the banks make the necessary adjustments? Our feeling is that the banks have already been making adjustments, and that given the opportunity, they will go on making these adjustments. If some liquidity is provided to support transactions taking place in the market, we will probably accomplish more on a broader basis than if the process were simply left as it was.

Some people ask what is in this for the banks. First, the banks were withdrawing from lending to these countries, and many of them are anxious to continue this process. If they do, they should do so in a way that provides some benefit to the debtor countries, which are, after all, their clients. And if this process can be concentrated within two or three years for those countries that are performing effectively, the banks will see their customers developing a stronger credit profile and gaining a greater probability of access once again to private markets.

The forty or fifty largest banks that have long-term relationships in the large debtor countries, either by direct representation in those markets or by a history of financing companies in those countries, will want to stay competitive vis-à-vis the other banks rather than withdraw entirely. That is one reason the impulse for new money will not, as is sometimes suggested, entirely dry up simply because there happens to be a greater emphasis on debt-reduction transactions that pass some benefit to the country.

If an appropriate balance is struck between the new money impulse and debt reduction and debt-service reduction, these two processes can go on simultaneously in the market as they have the past few years. If expectations are too high or if too much emphasis is placed on the debt reduction side, there is a danger that the new money impulse will be severely damaged. But that is a problem that the debtor countries, in designing their strategies with the banks, have to face. As they move into this period of negotiation, they will have to determine where to pitch that balance in order to do the two things they want: reduce the stock of debt and debt service; and at the same time ensure some future access to new money on a voluntary basis from the banks.

The main point is that we want to let the market function, instead of co-opting debt reduction or debt-service reduction into the international institutions or into some new facility specially designed to manage the process between the banks and the countries for the next thirty years. We do not think that is the way to go. The market has to be opened through the waiver process, and some financing is needed to support transactions. Then the market should be allowed to function, as we believe it will do efficiently if the parties can negotiate freely and transactions are agreed upon on a voluntary and market-oriented basis.

Meanwhile, the creditor governments will continue their support through the international institutions, the Paris Club, export financing, and so on. We will also review the regulatory, tax, and accounting areas to make sure that no unnecessary impediments stand in the way of future activity.

To sum up, three to four weeks of broad-based discussion took place around the world before the G-7 ministerial and the spring meetings took place. After the meetings, the G-7 communique was strongly positive. It endorsed not just the concepts but the specific proposals contained in the secretary's speech. That was repeated in the G-10 communique, in the IMF Interim Committee communique, and in the World Bank Development Committee communique. The breadth of response from creditors, debtors, international institutions, and commercial banks was very heartening. It was, of course, very general, and many details still had to be worked out. But it was impressive, and the speed with which we seem now to be moving is also impressive.

Commercial banks are examining their situation and have begun to meet with debtor countries. We have had conversations with them, and governments in other countries have had discussions with their commercial banks. Clearly, the banks are assessing the question of waivers and looking at the new proposals on the table. What appeared to be a demoralized situation a short time ago is now more positive. A positive dialogue is taking place, negotiations have begun, and momentum for constructive future negotiations has been gained.

13

Making the Best Use of Resources

A Discussion

QUESTION: In his speech, Secretary Brady used the term "loan guarantee." Why did you never use that word?

MR. MULFORD: I used the term "interest support." The word "guarantee" was used after the speech, but not in the speech. We never used that word, because we have in mind techniques to support interest flows without using the legal concept of a guarantee, both in the IMF and in the World Bank.

QUESTION: Regarding funds to be set aside in the World Bank and IMF to guarantee the interest obligation, do you or anyone else from the administration worry that you might have a replication of FSLIC's bankruptcy? In other words, you're creating a broad government insurance scheme supported by vastly underfunded pools?

MR. MULFORD: No, I don't. We are not setting aside these pools to guarantee. The concept is to use resources to support interest flows. There is a substantial difference.

If you have identified resources in one of the institutions that you believe should be used to support interest, those resources can be routed by virtue of a loan to the country, as opposed to a guarantee, which might go into an escrow account, where it would serve as potential backing under certain circumstances for interest of a certain magnitude for a certain period, say one year. Others, even the debtor country, might also contribute to that account to increase the resources. It is very important to determine the kind of techniques to accomplish these ends. It is just too simplistic to visualize guarantees, in which the IMF cannot legally engage anyway.

QUESTION: Isn't there a danger that you could end up with vastly underfunded escrow accounts?

Mr. MULFORD: I don't know what you mean by underfunded. The idea is simply to provide some support. If some interest support removes the 100 percent sovereign risk associated with those flows, the banks engaging in the transaction might participate more broadly. That is the purpose. It is not to assure the payment of all future interest.

QUESTION: I have a three-pronged question. First, one of the main issues here is that a consensus among the countries is necessary to solve the debt problem. It seems to me that after the IMF communique and the meetings in Spain, there is a divergence of views over how the whole debt issue should be structured by the preconditions of the Brady proposal. The presumptions that the countries should have a stabilization plan, that they should have a debt conversion program, and that they should not be in arrears are being contradicted by the IMF communique.

Second, what incentives will the banks have to continue new lending if they have to incur a write-down.

And, third, in all these discussions there is a certain confusion between debt reduction, which is stock reduction, and the debt-service reduction. If you take the $57.6 billion of Mexican public debt, cut it in half, and transact it for a bond, the interest reduction—once you issue the new bond as paid at LIBOR—is only $1.56 billion. I don't think that is what the Mexicans have in mind when they talk about a substantial debt reduction to decrease the debt service.

I think those three points are important. Would you like to comment on that?

Mr. MULFORD: I might comment on a couple, but I have already touched on some of them. The term "debt reduction" is difficult because people use it indiscriminately, without really meaning to. But when we use the term, we have in mind a transaction that has the effect of reducing in some way the stock of debt. That is all we have in mind. That could be a cash buyback, which extinguishes principal at a certain price. It could be the discount equivalent that is achieved in exchange of securities, collateralized such as the Mexicans did some time ago. But when we use that term, we only mean a reduction in the principal amount.

There is, as I said, some modest reduction in debt service that flows from reducing the stock of debt. But as I also said, that is not enough, so we are in agreement on that point and, I think, on the point you made about the Mexicans, that both are needed. Restructuring with interest rate write-down is needed. A classic case would be a so-called FASB 15 of the type used in this country by accountants to characterize a transaction where there is a restructuring of troubled debt, with an interest rate write-down, in such a way that the total flow of interest payments over

106

the life of the rescheduled principal amount equals the value of that nominal amount. In that case, a bank is able to treat that asset on its balance sheet as having a nominal value of par.

That is a very important concept. A bank that does not wish to take a principal write-down, but is willing to take some loss of earnings as part of its contribution to this situation, might find that a more appropriate transaction. If we provide resources to support one year of interest, with a relatively small amount of money we can accomplish a substantial decrease in debt service, though with no debt reduction. If we combine those two concepts and apply them in the market and provide resources for both, there is every chance that a fairly significant decrease in the stock of debt on the one hand, and in the debt service on the other, can be accomplished.

QUESTION: In that case, do you need some sort of contingency clause for the banks to have a recovery in the future?

MR. MULFORD: I haven't commented on that. I have simply said that was a matter for negotiation. Maybe there will be one; maybe there won't be. That is a question to be decided between the countries and their commercial banks. And the market will determine what the response to that issue should be.

We are not engaged in that part of the process. We are not writing this in detail with everybody's exact marching orders prescribed in detail, because banks may find that countries will agree after so many years to return to market rates. Or perhaps the rate cut today will be reduced in the future by a decline in interest rates, which means that the loss experienced by a bank in the future from a declining interest rate would be reduced. It could also grow, of course. A lot of points are up for negotiation.

QUESTION: Is that why you don't have consensus, because of the need to discuss the issue and the need for those contingency clauses, while time is passing, and the Mexicans are short of time?

MR. MULFORD: There is a consensus. We have seen it expressed publicly, and we know it in private. There is a significant consensus that the direction and concepts are right and are what the various parties are prepared to work with.

Obviously, a lot of negotiation has to be done, and some detailed decisions have to be made in the IMF and the World Bank. When the governments determine how our resources will be used, we have to know exactly the magnitude of resources and the rules by which they will be offered. Beyond that, we hope the market will function on those resources.

It will inevitably take time, but we hope the time will be short. Negotiations have already started between a number of countries and the banks, and, as I said, the institutions have made progress in addressing these problems. In a short time, I hope we will see a coming together of these things and significant progress, but there is a consensus.

QUESTION: As I understand it, the set-asides will be used to support debt reduction, and there will be a pool of funds to support debt-service reduction. If the markets overwhelmingly went for the latter because it provided more immediate relief for Mexico and, therefore, probably less of a hit implicit with the transaction, could the money that was set aside be used to support debt-service reduction?

MR. MULFORD: Our view is no, that the set-aside is to be used for debt reduction. And countries that agree to use debt reduction therefore unlock in the process the interest support mechanisms.

QUESTION: But wouldn't there be a lot more bang for the dollar?

MR. MULFORD: Not necessarily. What is important both politically and economically and for both the creditor and the debtor nations is that some effort be made to reduce the stock of debt, or at least to prevent the stock of debt from continually rising into the future.

If that is not a concern for some reason, then the people engaged must think it will never be paid back. No one can be insensitive to a constant and endless accumulation of debt and ultimately debt service, with the impact that has on transfer payments and so on.

Addressing the problem of the stock of debt must have a high priority, but we do not want to be dogmatic about it. The market needs both transactions. Each specific situation will be different, because each country will probably plan to accomplish more of one than the other. Some countries will have a strong preference for debt-service reduction, although they also want some debt reduction, and others will prefer debt reduction.

The same is true of the banks. In the United States, certain banks in certain circumstances for certain kinds of debtors may prefer to take principal losses. Others may want interest write-down, certain banks may want a blend. So both have to be done, but debt reduction is an important part of the concept.

QUESTION: Someone spoke of a consensus in which the international organizations and some countries were already willing to put some money into debt reduction, and Japan was said to be willing to put more exports into debt reduction. Would you care to comment about Japan's role within the plan?

MR. MULFORD: The Japanese have agreed to support the concepts and proposals that were tabled, and they are working closely with us to see them implemented. They also indicated a willingness to channel their own resources on a parallel basis with the international institutions and linked to debt-reduction programs.

They have not agreed specifically to put their resources into the pool that reduces debt or the pool that supports interest payments. But they have made an important proposed contribution. Although the flows may come from Ex-Im Bank in Japan, they will to some extent offset the effect of the set-aside from the institutions, funds that are not immediately usable by the debtor countries. So the money is fungible, but an important ingredient. We welcome their participation.

QUESTION: Have they emphasized any specific conditionality?

MR. MULFORD: They strongly emphasize general conditionality in the IMF and the World Bank. They would not be willing to engage in those flows unless appropriate Fund and Bank conditionality were in place.

QUESTION: You haven't said anything about the U.S. interest in all this. Why is the U.S. government involved? Nobody has said anything about that except that we want to keep some unemployed Mexicans from coming across the border. I'm not suggesting that there is no national interest, but it seems to me that if you say something about the nature and the intensity of that interest, it is hard to say anything about the nature and degree of the U.S. government's involvement in it.

MR. MULFORD: We have had a lengthy period of adjustment since the debt crisis first appeared in 1982. I use the word "adjustment" in a broad sense. Over that time, the countries have had to recognize that the adjustment of their policies and the need to reform and so on will not be just a momentary pulling in of the belt, after which we can go back to business as usual. It took a considerable period for the realities of the adjustment to be embraced by the countries.

The same was true of the creditor governments and the institutions. We all had to go through that process. We had an international financial system and a banking system that was fragile and exposed to the threat the international debt crisis appeared to pose to the international payment system and to the financial system in general.

The effort made in 1985 to strengthen the strategy emphasized the need for growth and reform and for giving countries hope that if they moved in that direction they could work their way out of the problem. The international financial system was better off by that time but not fully strengthened and not without some risks. That situation prevailed for several years, but now, I think, we are entering a phase when the international financial system and the banks are in a much stronger position. The institutions have a lot more experience, but their contribution appeared, in the end, to be increasing the stock of debt, a solution that in the long term did not seem practical.

There was a growing awareness of the political costs and the long-term geopolitical considerations for the United States of not addressing this problem, which has more dimensions than the economic and financial. The most important point is to recognize the need of an approach that strengthens the strategy by acknowledging the need for countries to reduce their debt burdens and their debt-service payments, especially if they have already made reforms and are committed to continuing in that direction.

We think there could be big dividends. Over a period of three years, a number of countries might actually graduate back into using world markets effectively. Then they would no longer be part of the debt problem in the same way. That would represent a significant breakthrough.

QUESTION: Do you feel that debt-equity swaps are still part of a debt-relief program? And if so, are they needed? And is any benefit involved for Mexico or other indebted countries?

MR. MULFORD: I use the term debt-reduction program rather than debt-relief program. We continue to believe that debt-equity swaps are very important. Countries that have had a commitment to open up to investment and to encourage investment and that have been willing to set their other policy priorities to accommodate a debt-equity swap program have been highly successful. Chile is perhaps the leading example.

There are also problems that have to be managed with debt-equity programs, but a country has to be willing to take account in other policy areas of the need for adjustments to accommodate debt-equity programs. That means they need to have a strong willingness to encourage investment, including foreign direct investment.

Countries may feel negative because they do not want to make those priority judgments or to welcome foreign investment. Mexico has raised certain objections to us, and we listened carefully. We are aware that they have a more limited concept in mind, but we have also heard that it is a question of timing. In due course, debt-equity swaps may play a bigger role in the field.

Although the matter is still under discussion, we remain convinced that debt-equity swap programs are important. They are an important indicator of the view toward investment. Debt-reduction cannot be said to be regarded seriously in countries that do not use all means to accomplish it, so we think debt-for-equity swaps continue to be important.

QUESTION: I agree thoroughly about the political desirability of an initiative of the United States. My question regards the perception of Secretary Brady's initiative. There is some concern about its not being considered a bailout. How would you comment on that?

MR. MULFORD: That is an important point, because it is clear that the proposals do not constitute a bank bailout. We do not visualize additional resources being put into the two institutions at this time in order to carry out these proposals. These are resources that are already in use. They have already been put there, and they are being used for these purposes today, as they have been in the past and will be in the future.

The question is: How can they be used more effectively? Our judgment is that a portion should be used to reduce debt and debt service instead of to build debt. That is the first answer.

The second answer is that, however it is structured, the debt-reduction transaction, with an exchange of securities collateralized, takes place at a substantial discount. The communiques that were issued used the term "substantial debt reduction." If official resources are used to support collateralization and limited interest, they will be used only when there is a substantial reduction in principal. That means a substantial loss accepted and recorded by a bank.

On the interest rate reduction, we are talking about a transaction where the interest rate is written down, but the principal is not collateralized. Therefore, the official support is used only to support the resulting reduced interest rate. So again the bank has to agree to take a substantial hit in earnings if it accepts that. Therefore, I don't see how they can be characterized as bank bailouts.

QUESTION: Is there an offset according to accounting?

MR. MULFORD: Well, there may be some tax advantage for certain banks at certain times, but they can never cover the full magnitude of the hit.

QUESTION: Can you give us some idea what portion of the total debt you think can be reduced, and what portion of the total service requirement?

MR. MULFORD: This question keeps coming up, and I don't believe it is very constructive, for reasons that have to do with the variety of assumptions that have to be made. The assumptions cover things like future interest rate movements; the depth of discounts and markets; whether market prices go up or go down as debt reduction begins; the kinds of deals struck with the banks; whether the countries take the reforms necessary to unlock the resources for this purpose; and so on. We went through that exercise in order to make some rough calculation of the potential resource use in the institutions. It was an important exercise. To try to deduce from those numbers the total effect on debt and debt service might be interesting but is not really germane to the ultimate result.

I would suggest that we focus on individual country cases and try to determine the impact that can be made in each case on both debt and debt-service reduction. In my testimony, I indicated that we did not think it beyond possibility to see an approximately 20 percent reduction in debt and debt service and in some cases more. With debt-equity swap programs in place, that might be a higher figure. So we will be focusing on individual country cases to see what kind of result we can bring.

QUESTION: I understand why there is a lot of emphasis on debt and debt-service reduction, but why so little on new money?

MR. MULFORD: The debt and debt-service reduction proposals have attracted the greatest interest. Because they are new and they are rather complex in certain details, they tend to be discussed most.

I did say that new money is an essential part of the exercise and will continue to be so. New money takes many forms. We use the term "new money" for concerted lending packages negotiated by bank advisory committees. When I use it, however, I have in mind trade finance, bank lines, project finance, and club loans used to top off a particular transaction, as was done recently in Colombia—and I am not excluding concerted lending. The debtors and the banks will have to discuss these issues as they look at the total financing need, the resources available, what debt reduction and debt-service reduction can be accomplished, what might be accomplished in capital repatriation and investment flows, and finally what portion might be accounted for by new money in its various forms. We understand that it is part of the negotiations, and we place great emphasis on the need for continuing new money flows.

QUESTION: Could you comment on the free rider issue? Do you see the program being jeopardized by some banks refraining from participation in the hopes that the ones that go first will raise the market values?

MR. MULFORD: The number of free riders is fairly large, and they are an irritating problem for the banks. But they do not account for a significant portion of the finance. In my judgment, since the free rider problem is an extremely difficult problem to solve and only soluble, perhaps, at the cost of upsetting financial flows, it should be set aside for the moment. Most major banks will want to move forward and participate in these proposals, rather than become free riders.

Unless that situation changes, the right answer is not to place too much emphasis on it. Over time, free riders will be distinguished, because if they do not participate, they will not enjoy any of the enhancements. If they do not participate in the debt-reduction transaction, they will not get a collateralized piece of paper, for example, or supported interest flows. Over time, that may make a difference.

Appendix
Third World Debt

Nicholas F. Brady

More than forty years ago, the representatives of forty-four nations met at Bretton Woods, New Hampshire, to build a new international economic and financial system. The lessons learned from a devastating world depression and global conflict guided their efforts. At the concluding session, the president of the conference, Treasury Secretary Henry Morgenthau, described this lesson in the following manner:

> We have come to recognize that the wisest and most effective way to protect our national interests is through international cooperation—this is to say, through united effort for the attainment of common goals. This has been the great lesson of contemporary life—that the peoples of the earth are inseparably linked to one another by a deep, underlying community of purpose.

The enduring legacy provided by the Bretton Woods institutions is lasting testament to the success of their efforts. This community of purpose still resides in these institutions today. We must once again draw on this special sense of purpose as we renew our efforts to create and foster world growth.

These past seven years we have faced a major challenge in the international debt problem. This situation is, in fact, a complex accumulation of a myriad of interwoven problems. It contains economic, political, and social elements. Taken together, they represent a truly international problem, for which no one set of actions or circumstances is responsible. And for which no one nation can provide the solution. Ultimately, resolution depends on a great cooperative effort by the international community. It requires the mobilization of the world's

---

Remarks by Secretary of the Treasury Nicholas F. Brady to the Brookings Institution and the Bretton Woods Committee Conference on Third World Debt, March 10, 1989.

resources and the dedication of its goodwill.

Since 1982 the world community has endeavored to come to terms with international debt. In 1985 we paused and took stock of our progress in addressing the problem. As a result of that review, together we brought forth a new strategy, centered on economic growth. This still makes sense. However, it is appropriate that now, almost four years later, we again take stock. Thus in recent months we have undertaken to look afresh at the international debt situation. The purpose was to discover what progress has been made: to see where we as a community of nations have succeeded and where we have not. And, where our success has not met our expectations, to understand why we have not achieved our goals. We have studied in depth, we have consulted widely—seeking and taking into account the views of debtor nations, multilateral institutions, commercial banks, and legislatures. We have also consulted closely with Japan and other industrial countries in order to begin to lay the basis for a common approach to the debt problem by the creditor countries.

Let me share with you the results of our reassessment as part of the ongoing process of international collaboration. I would hope that the ideas and suggestions I put forth here will provide a basis for a concerted effort by the international community to reinvigorate a process that has become debt-weary. However, we must strengthen the process without stopping it. As we move ahead with these ideas in the weeks ahead, it is important to continue working on individual debt problems.

Recent Progress

Our review confirmed that we have accomplished much, but much remains to be done.

The experience of the past four years demonstrates that the fundamental principles of the current strategy remain sound:

- Growth is essential to the resolution of debt problems.
- Debtor nations will not achieve sufficient levels of growth without reform.
- Debtor nations have a continuing need for external resources.
- Solutions must be undertaken on a case-by-case basis.

In recent years, we have seen positive growth occur in many debtor nations. Last year six major debtor nations realized more than 4 percent positive growth. This is primarily due to the debtors' own efforts. The political leadership of many of these nations has demonstrated their commitment to implement vital macroeconomic and structural reforms. In many countries this has been reflected in the privatization of nationalized industries. In some countries there has also been a move toward opening their shores to greater foreign trade and investment. Current account deficits have been sharply reduced, and the portion of export earnings going to pay interest on external debt has declined. These are significant achievements. All the more so, since in parallel progress, a number of debtor nations have advanced toward more democratic regimes. This has required great courage and persistence. The people of these countries have made substantial sacrifices for which they've earned our admiration. We must work together to transform these sacrifices into tangible and lasting benefits.

In another positive development, we have avoided a major disruption to the global payments system. Commercial banks have strengthened their capital and built reserves, placing them in a stronger position to contribute to a more rapid resolution of debt problems. The "menu" approach of the current strategy has helped to sustain new financial support while also encouraging debt reduction efforts. The banks have provided loans in support of debtor country economic programs. The stock of debt in the major debtor countries has been reduced by some $24 billion in the past two years through various voluntary debt reduction techniques.

However, despite the accomplishments to date, we must acknowledge that serious problems and impediments to a successful resolution of the debt crisis remain. Clearly, in many of the major debtor nations, growth has not been sufficient. Nor has the level of economic policy reform been adequate. Capital flight has drained resources from debtor nations' economies. Meanwhile, neither investment nor domestic savings have shown much improvement. In many cases, inflation has not been brought under control. Commercial bank lending has not always been timely. The force of these circumstances has overshadowed the progress achieved. Despite progress, prosperity remains, but for many, out of reach.

Other pressures also exist. The multilateral institutions and the Paris Club have made up a portion of the shortfall in finance. Commercial bank exposure to the major debtors since 1985 has declined slightly, while the exposure of the international institutions has increased sharply. If this trend were to continue, it could lead to a situation in which the debt problem would be transferred largely to the international institutions, weakening their financial position.

These are realities that we cannot deny. They are problems we must address if we are to renew progress on the international debt crisis.

Let me reiterate that we believe that the fundamental principles of the current strategy remain valid. However, we believe that the time has come for all members of the international community to consider new ways that they may contribute to the common effort.

In considering next steps, a few key points should be kept in mind:

• First, obviously financial resources are scarce. Can they be used more effectively?

• Second, we must recognize that reversing capital flight offers a major opportunity, since in many cases flight capital is larger than outstanding debt.

• Third, there is no substitute for sound policies.

• Fourth, we must maintain the important role of the international financial institutions and preserve their financial integrity.

•Fifth, we should encourage debt and debt-service reduction on a voluntary basis, while recognizing the importance of continued new lending. This should provide an important step back to the free markets, where funds abound and transactions are enacted in days not months.

•Finally, we must draw together these elements to provide debtor countries with greater hope for the future.

Strengthening the Current Strategy

Any new approach must continue to emphasize the importance of stronger growth in debtor nations, as well as the need for debtor reforms and adequate financial support to achieve that growth. We will have success only if our efforts are truly cooperative. And, to succeed we must have the commitment and involvement of all parties.

First and foremost, debtor nations must focus particular attention on the adoption of policies which can better encourage new investment flows, strengthen domestic savings, and promote the return of flight capital. This requires sound growth policies which foster confidence in both domestic and foreign investors. These are essential ingredients for reducing the future stock of debt and sustaining strong growth. Specific policy measures in these areas should be part of any new IMF and World Bank programs. It is worth noting that total capital flight for most major debtors is roughly comparable to their total debt.

Second, the creditor community—banks, international financial institutions, and creditor governments—should provide more effective and timely financial support. A number of steps are needed in this area.

Commercial banks need to work with debtor nations to provide a broader range of alternatives for financial support, including greater efforts to achieve both debt and debt-service reduction and to provide new lending. The approach to this problem must be realistic. The path toward greater creditworthiness and a return to the markets for many debtor countries needs to involve debt reduction. Diversified forms of financial support need to flourish and constraints should be relaxed. To be specific, the sharing and negative pledge clauses included in existing loan agreements are a substantial barrier to debt reduction. In addition, the banking community's interests have become more diverse in recent years. This needs to be recognized by both banks and debtors to take advantage of various preferences.

A key element of this approach, therefore, would be the negotiation of a general waiver of the sharing and negative pledge clauses for each performing debtor, to permit an orderly process whereby banks which wish to do so negotiate debt or debt-service reduction transactions. Such waivers might have a three-year life, to stimulate activity within a short but measurable time frame. We expect these waivers to accelerate sharply the pace of debt reduction and pass the benefits directly to the debtor nation. We would expect debtor nations also to maintain viable debt/equity swap programs for the duration of this endeavor, and would encourage them to permit domestic nationals to engage in such transactions.

Of course, banks will remain interested in providing new money, especially if creditworthiness improves over the three year period. They should be encouraged to do so, for new financing will still be required. In this connection, consideration could be given in some cases to ways of differentiating new from old debt.

The international financial institutions will need to continue to play central roles. The heart of their effort would be to promote sound policies in the debtor countries through advice and financial support. With steady performance under IMF and World Bank programs, these institutions can catalyze new financing. In addition, to support and encourage debtor and commercial bank efforts to reduce debt and debt-service burdens, the IMF and World Bank could provide funding, as part of their policy-based lending programs, for debt or debt service reduction purposes. This financial support would be available to countries which elect to undertake a debt reduction program. A portion of their policy-based loans could be used to finance specific debt reduction plans. These funds could support collateralized debt for bond exchanges involving a significant discount on outstanding debt. They could also be used to replenish reserves following a cash buyback.

Moreover, both institutions could offer new, additional financial support to collateralize a portion of interest payments for debt or debt-service reduction transactions. By offering direct financial support for debt and debt-service operations, the IMF and the World Bank could provide new incentives, which would act simultaneously to strengthen prospects for greater creditworthiness and to restore voluntary private financing in the future. This could lead to considerable improvements in the cash flow positions of the debtor countries.

While the IMF and World Bank will want to set guidelines on how their funds are used, the negotiation of transactions will remain in the marketplace—encouraged and supported but not managed by the international institutions.

It will be important that the fund and the bank both be in a strong financial postion to fulfill effectively their roles in the strengthened strategy. The Bretton Woods Committee has provided an important public service in mobilizing capital resources for these institutions. The capital of the World Bank has recently been replenished with the implementation of the recent general capital increase providing approximately $75 billion in new resources to the bank. With respect to the fund, the implementation of these new efforts to strengthen the debt strategy could help lay the basis for an increase in IMF quotas. There are, of course, other important issues that have to be addressed in the quota review, including the IMF arrears problem and a need for clear vision of the IMF's role in the 1990s. It is our hope that a consensus can be reached on the quota question before the end of the year.

Creditor governments should continue to reschedule or restructure their own exposure through the Paris Club, and to maintain export credit cover for countries with sound reform programs. In addition, creditor countries which are in a position to provide additional financing in support of this effort may wish to consider doing so. This could contribute significantly to the overall success of this effort. We believe that creditor governments should also consider how to reduce regulatory, accounting, or tax impediments to debt reduction, where these exist.

The third key element of our thinking involves more timely and flexible financial support. The current manner in which "financial gaps" are estimated and filled is cumbersome and rigid. We should seek to change this mentality and make the process work better. At the same time, we must maintain the close association between economic performance and external financial support.

While we believe the IMF should continue to estimate debtor financing needs, we question whether the international financial institutions should delay their initial disbursements until firm, detailed commitments have been provided by all other creditors to fill the financing "gap." In many instances, this has served to provide a false sense of security rather than meaningful financial support. The banks will themselves need to provide diverse, active, and timely support in order to facilitate servicing of the commercial debt remaining after debt reduction. Debtor nations should set goals for both new investment and the repatriation of flight capital, and to adopt policy measures designed to achieve those targets. Debtor nations and commercial banks should determine through negotiations the portion of financing needs to be met via concerted or voluntary lending; and the contribution to be made by voluntary debt or debt-service reduction.

Finally, sound policies and open, growing markets within the industrial nations will continue to be an essential foundation for efforts to make progress on the debt problem. We cannot reasonably expect the debtor nations to increase their exports and strengthen their economies without access to industrial country markets. The Uruguay Round of trade negotiations provides an important opportunity to advance an open trading system. We must all strive to make this a success.

Conclusion

Taken together, the ideas I have discussed today represent a basis on which we can work to revitalize the current debt strategy. We believe that through our efforts we can provide substantial benefits for debtor nations in the form of more manageable debt service obligations, smaller and more realistic financing needs, stronger economic growth, and higher standards of living for their people.

If we work together, we can make important progress toward our key objectives:

- to assure that benefits are available to any debtor nation which demonstrates a commitment to sound policies
- to minimize the cost or contingent shift in risk to creditor governments and taxpayers
- to provide maximum opportunities for voluntary, market-based transactions rather than mandatory centralization of debt restructurings
- and to better tap the potential for alternative sources of private capital

In the final analysis, our objective is to rekindle the hope of the people and leaders of debtor nations that their sacrifices will lead to greater prosperity in the present and the prospect of a future unclouded by the burden of debt.

Notes

CHAPTER 2: DEVELOPING-COUNTRY DEBT PROBLEMS AFTER SEVEN YEARS

1. *Washington Post*, January 11, 1989.

CHAPTER 3: REDUCING TRANSFERS FROM DEBTOR COUNTRIES

1. This section draws on Rudiger Dornbusch, "Policy and Perform-ance Linkages between LDC Debtors and Industrial Countries," Brook-ings Papers on Economic Activity, no. 2 (Washington, D.C.: Brookings Institution, 1985).

2. The fact that it is often food subsidies that are eliminated, without the proverbial neutral lump sum tax to compensate the losers, does not seem to limit the case for the policy recommendation.

3. Not shown are various Central and South American countries, Yugoslavia, Nigeria, and the Ivory Coast.

4. For an extensive discussion, see John Williamson, *Voluntary Approaches to Debt Reduction* (Washington, D.C.: Institute for International Economics, 1988).

5. It is readily verified that the debt-to-GDP ratio evolves according to $\Delta b = (r - y) b - \sigma$ where r and y are the real interest rate and the growth rate of output and σ is the noninterest current account surplus. (It is assumed that direct investment income is offset by capital flight.) With a debt ratio of 60 percent and a real interest rate less growth of 5 percent, the noninterest surplus has to be 3 percent of GDP to avoid a rising debt ratio.

6. Jeremy Bulow and Kenneth Rogoff, "The Buyback Boondoggle," Brookings Papers on Economic Activity, no. 2 (Washington, D.C.: Brookings Institution, 1988).

7. On this point see especially Michael Dooley, "Buy-Backs and Market Valuation," IMF Staff Papers (Washington, D.C.: International Monetary Fund, 1988).

8. See W. Buiter and T. N. Srinivasan, "Rewarding the Profligate and Punishing the Prudent and Poor: Some Recent Proposals for Debt Relief," *World Development*, vol. 15, no. 3 (1987), pp. 411–17.

CHAPTER 4: MARKET-BASED APPROACHES TO DEBT REDUCTION

1. Jeremy Bulow and Kenneth Rogoff, "The Buyback Boondoggle," Brookings Papers on Economic Activity, no. 2 (Washington, D.C.:

Brookings Institution, 1988).

2. John Williamson, *Voluntary Approaches to Debt Relief* (Washington, D.C.: Institute for International Economics, 1988).

3. Bulow and Rogoff, "The Buyback Boondoggle."

4. For detailed calculations, see Ruben Lamdany, "Bolivia, Mexico, and Beyond" (Washington, D.C.: World Bank, 1988).

5. For a discussion of the budgetary issues, see Paul Krugman, "Market-based Debt Reduction Schemes," in J. Frenkel, ed., *Analytics of International Debt* (Washington, D.C.: International Monetary Fund, forthcoming).

Index

Additionality concept, 61–62
Adjustment to debt, 22–28
Affiliate. *See* Debt facility; International financial institutions; Loan guarantee, market value
Appropriability concept, 45, 54–56
Argentina, 1, 3, 10–11, 15, 16, 36, 38

Baker, James A., III, 4, 10, 11
Baker plan, 1; effect and problems of, 4, 71–73, 79–80; elements of strategy to implement, 75–76; validity of, 99
Bearer bonds, 67–68
Bentsen, Lloyd, 80
Bolivia, 54
Brady, Nicholas, 5, 9–10, 11, 57
Brady plan: advantage of, 65; bank evaluation of proposals in, 83–86; country and agency support for, 103; debt buyback strategy under, 44; elements and weakness of, 5, 21; as evolution of Baker plan, 75–76; final form lacking, 5, 10, 20, 71–72; market value guarantee as component of, 44, 71–72; philosophy of, 103; as presumed bailout, 67, 111; private and official mixture for debt problem, 1–2; problems of and proposals for, 71–73; proposal for financing and additional contributions under, 76–78, 91; scenarios for elements of proposed, 57–60; sharing and negative pledge clauses in, 72, 118; text of, 115–21
Brazil: debt conversion financing in, 35; decline in debt's market value, 10–11; economic and political problems in, 1, 2–3, 17, 72
Budget, public sector: debt-service problems of, 26–28; effect of spending cuts on investment, 28; as source of debt problem, 37–38
Bulow, Jeremy, 34, 48, 55
Burden sharing, 13–14
Bush, George, 10, 83

Capital flight: conditions for reversal of, 28, 33, 40; effect of, 10, 27–29, 33; need to solve problem of, 73, 78; reduction in Mexico of, 81
Chile: economic stabilization in, 2; sustained market value of debt of, 10;

use of buyback strategy by, 34
Colombia, 2, 36, 38, 85
Commercial banks: debt exposure dilution by, 4, 10, 12, 14, 17; debt exposure relative to official agencies, 15, 98; debtor country obligations to, 9, 15–16; effect of hypothetical market value guarantee on, 19; effect of reduced market value of loans by, 17–19; evaluation of Brady plan proposals by, 83–86; presumed reaction to interest recycling by, 39–40; response to proposed Brady plan, 103
Competition in trade, 25–26, 28
Creditors: and appropriability, 54–56; benefit of externally financed buyback to, 48; effect of debt swap on, 49–53; effect of domestic repurchase scheme on, 55–57; effect of proposed Brady plan on, 72; sharing and negative pledge clauses and, 72. *See also* Commercial banks; Industrialized countries; Official agencies

Debt, developing country: decline in market value of, 10, 17–19, 22, 43; effect of burden on country's ability to repay, 51–53; effect on commercial banks of exposure to, 9, 14–15, 17–19
Debt buybacks: cost of, 47; domestically financed, 53–57; externally financed, 45, 46–49, 53; as means for debt reduction, 33–37, 43–44; types of, 44
Debt crisis, 1982, 1; lending and borrowing experience before and after, 23; reasons for debt-service problems, 2
Debt-equity swaps, 43, 60–63, 84–85, 110–11
Debt facility or affiliate, proposed, 12–14, 66–67. *See also* International financial institutions; Loan guarantee, market value
Debt Laffer curve analysis, 52, 53, 58, 59
Debtor countries: adjustment to debt by, 22–28, 67, 75–76; argument for debt reduction of, 12; debt characteristics of, 30–31; economic decline in, 3, 21; economic reform in, 67, 73, 75, 78, 88; external debt of, 15; incidence of, 87; increasing lack of creditworthiness, 10, 17; loans for debt-service payments to,

9; ratio of debt to GDP, 31–32, 33; reform to encourage capital return in, 72–73; secondary market discount for debt of, 43; trade or fiscal problems of, 37–38; trade surpluses in, 3. *See also* Commercial banks; Debt service; International financial institutions; Official agencies

Debt reduction: benefits, 46; with cash financing, 44–45; choice of principal or interest for, 37; costs and benefits of buyback strategy for, 34–35; instruments for, 33–41; proposals for, 32; strategies for, 31. *See also* Debt buybacks.

Debt restructuring, 99–100, 106–7

Debt service: causes of problem in, 32; complications of adjustment to, 23–28; effect of forced, 24–26; loans to debtor countries to pay, 9; and problems of public sector budget, 26; reasons for problems of, 2; resource transfer effect of, 22–24; restructure effect of, 37–38; since debt crisis of 1982, 3. *See also* Interest recycling

Debt swaps: experience of Mexico with, 50, 56–57; as instruments to reduce debt, 33; and seniority of new debt, 49–53. *See also* Seniority of debt

Europe, 31

Exchange rate: effect of devaluation of, 27, 28; effect of using reserves for debt reduction, 35

Fiscal policy: reform required for debt management, 32, 33. *See also* Budget, public sector; Mexico; Spending reduction effect

Foreign exchange: issue interacts with budget problem, 27; need for debtor countries to earn dollars in, 24–26

Free rider problem, 113

Government intervention, 93

Guarantees. *See* Loan guarantee, market value

Incentive effect concept, 45

Incentives, 5, 71

Industrialized countries: cooperation in debt-reduction problem, 13, 94–95; as creditors, 39–40, 77; support vehicles of, 102

Inflation: effect of high, 14; financing of, 10; in Latin America, 15–17; measures to lower, 15; as outcome of forced debt service, 27

Interest rates, real, 15, 27

Interest recycling, 37–40

Interest support concept, 102, 105–6

Interest transfer problem, 22–26

International financial institutions: competing demands for resources of, 66; proposal for affiliate or debt facility for, 12–14, 66–67. *See also* International Monetary Fund (IMF); World Bank

International Monetary Fund (IMF): increase in loans by, 15; Japan's request for increased representation in, 13–14; loan repayment priority of, 9; role under proposed Brady plan, 77–78, 99

Investment, 24, 28

Japan: contributed funds for debt reduction, 76; participation in lending to debtor countries, 31; as possible funder of debt facility, 13–14, 109

Kissinger, Henry, 11

Korea, 72

Latin America: decline in living standard in, 21, 23. *See also* Argentina; Brazil; Chile; Debtor countries; Mexico

Loan guarantee, market value: as component of Brady plan, 44, 58–60, 105; disproportionate bank gains with, 19; flaw in Brady plan proposal for, 71–72; proposal for development bank affiliate for, 66–67; for reliable debt service by debtor countries, 12; scenarios without implementation of, 21. *See also* Interest support concept

Loans: for debt service, 9; effect on commercial banks of losses, 10, 17–19; market value of, 9, 10, 12, 14, 15–19

Macroeconomic issues, 23–28

Marxism, 11, 14

Mexico: budget balance in, 3, 32, 91–92; debt of, 1; debt swap experience of, 49, 56–57; economic growth and privatization in, 79; effect of buyback strategy for, 34, 35; effect of import liberalization on trade surplus of, 4–5; stabilization of debt's market value, 16–17

Miyazawa, Kiichi, 13

Moral hazard problem, 19

Mulford, David, 5

New money, 3–4, 85, 100, 102, 112

Official agencies: debt and debt service reduction strategy of, 92; debtor country obligations to, 15; increased

lending exposure of, 3–4, 98–99; lending to service debt by, 9
Opening of economy. *See* Mexico

Paris Club, 98, 103
Perez, Carlos Andres, 16
Peru, 3, 10–11
Politics of debt, 11, 14, 65
Populism, 3, 11, 14
Privatization, 79
Public sector: fiscal problems in debtor countries of, 26–28. *See also* Budget, public sector

Reed, John, 9, 10
Regan, Donald, 10
Risk in lending, 67, 99
Rogoff, Kenneth, 34, 48, 55

Secondary market: domestic debt repurchase on, 54; effect of externally financed buyback on price on, 47; effect on price with new senior debt, 50; price of debt on, 22, 46
Seniority of debt, 49–54, 57–58, 59–60
Set-aside: of debt loss revenues by Citicorp, 10; use of concept of, 101, 108
Sharing and negative pledge clauses, 72, 118
Spending reduction effect, 23–28

Swaps. *See* Debt-equity swaps; Debt swaps

Trade: as source of debt problem, 37–38; surplus, 5
Transfer problem. *See* Budget, public sector; Debt service; Foreign exchange; Spending reduction effect

Uncertainty, 46
United States: effect of Treasury policies on lending, 3–4; fiscal problems in, 95; participation in lending to debtor countries, 31

Venezuela: debt problems of, 16–17; decline in debt's market value, 10–11
Volcker, Paul A., 4

Wages/employment, 25–27
Welfare effects: for domestic financing of debt buyback, 55; of external financing for debt swaps, 51–53; of externally financed buyback, 47–48; of swapping old for new senior debt, 51
World Bank: increase in loans by, 15; Japan's request for increased representation in, 13–14; loan repayment priority of, 9; role under proposed Brady plan, 77–78, 100
Wriston, Walter, 93

A Note on the Book

This book was edited by the publications staff
of the American Enterprise Institute.
The figures were drawn by Hördur Karlsson,
and the index was prepared by Shirley Kessel.
The text was set in Palatino, a typeface designed by Hermann Zapf.
Mount Vernon Printing Company, of Landover, Maryland,
set the type, and printed and bound the book,
using permanent, acid-free paper.